Into the Pilgrimverse

Into the Pilgrimverse

Contemporary Reception and Adaptation
of *The Pilgrim's Progress*

ANDY DRAYCOTT

⌒PICKWICK *Publications* · Eugene, Oregon

INTO THE PILGRIMVERSE
Contemporary Reception and Adaptation of *The Pilgrim's Progress*

Copyright © 2025 Andy Draycott. All rights reserved. Except for brief quotations in critical publications or reviews, no part of this book may be reproduced in any manner without prior written permission from the publisher. Write: Permissions, Wipf and Stock Publishers, 199 W. 8th Ave., Suite 3, Eugene, OR 97401.

Pickwick Publications
An Imprint of Wipf and Stock Publishers
199 W. 8th Ave., Suite 3
Eugene, OR 97401

www.wipfandstock.com

PAPERBACK ISBN: 978-1-6667-4872-7
HARDCOVER ISBN: 978-1-6667-4873-4
EBOOK ISBN: 978-1-6667-4874-1

Cataloguing-in-Publication data:

Names: Draycott, Andy, author.

Title: Into the pilgrimverse : contemporary reception and adaptation of *The Pilgrim's Progress* / Andy Draycott.

Description: Eugene, OR : Pickwick Publications, 2025 | Includes bibliographical references.

Identifiers: ISBN 978-1-6667-4872-7 (paperback) | ISBN 978-1-6667-4873-4 (hardcover) | ISBN 978-1-6667-4874-1 (ebook)

Subjects: LCSH: Bunyan, John, 1628–1688. Pilgrim's progress. | Pilgrim's progress (Bunyan, John). | Bunyan, John, 1628–1688—Influence. | Christian literature, English—History and criticism.

Classification: PR3330.A9 .D73 2025 (paperback) | PR3330.A9 (ebook)

VERSION NUMBER 071625

Scriptures taken from the Holy Bible, New International Version®, NIV®. Copyright © 1973, 1978, 1984, 2011 by Biblica, Inc.™ Used by permission of Zondervan. All rights reserved worldwide. www.zondervan.com The "NIV" and "New International Version" are trademarks registered in the United States Patent and Trademark Office by Biblica, Inc.™

Lyrics from A Prayer for Pilgrims ©1998 Kenneth A. Puls. Used by Permission. kenpulsmusic.com.

Contents

1 Introduction | 1

2 Books | 20

3 Comics | 42

4 Church | 66

5 Home | 89

6 Sounds | 113

7 Sights | 135

8 Margins | 158

9 Conclusion | 181

Acknowledgments | 191

1

Introduction

> Now faith is confidence in what we hope for and assurance about what we do not see. This is what the ancients were commended for. By faith we understand that the universe was formed at God's command, so that what is seen was not made out of what was visible.
>
> HEBREWS 11:1–3

This book records conversations between characters, most of whom emerge from the pages of John Bunyan's *The Pilgrim" Progress*, both Part I (1678) and Part II (1684). Others are drawn from adaptations and performances based on the book. As you will see, their dwelling place, and the site of their adventures, is the Pilgrimverse. Each chapter is a record of reports provided from expeditions to some particular area of the Pilgrimverse as indicated by the chapter title. To help you in reading the reports, please find below short introductions to each of the book's characters, given in the order of their appearance. This little guide and introduction will also serve to point you to any chapter that you prefer to jump to out of order.

Narrator (NAR): As author of this book, the Narrator is a middle-aged, white, male, immigrant scholar living and teaching theology in Southern California in the US. He shares his Christian faith with John Bunyan, and its formation and expression mark him out as an evangelical. With ultimate control over the book flow, the Narrator intervenes to draw out the significance of conversations and to sum up each discussion topic for the sake of chapter divisions. He chooses the Bible verses that head up each chapter and is tasked to keep things on track. He functions as a voice from above and no one in the book ever sees him, even though, in his dreams, he sees all of them.

Researcher (RES): He recruits the explorers for each Pilgrimverse expedition and receives their reports. It is amid the piles of Pilgrim's Progress paraphernalia perilously perched on his office desk that portals to the Pilgrimverse are discovered and accessed. He's interested in really nerdy details and could bore for hours on many things touched on here, and has done so not only in academic articles, but also in his classroom filled with his students as well. It is in aid of his research that the rest of the characters from *The Pilgrim's Progress* explore the Pilgrimverse.

Faithful (FAI): A neighbor of Christian's from the City of Destruction who, in Part I, serves as his first companion. Faithful overtakes Christian by not hanging out at the Palace Beautiful. Their subsequent meeting is a great piece of slapstick comedy. He's not Christian's forever companion on account of his being detained, charged, tried, convicted and burned at the stake at Vanity Fair.

Hopeful (HOP): Brought to faith by Faithful's testimony, Hopeful leaves Vanity, and joins Christian for the rest of his journey, effectively becoming a buddy replacement for Faithful. His testimony of coming to faith is closest to John Bunyan's own account in his spiritual autobiography *Grace Abounding*. In adaptations, Hopeful receives, for whatever reason, the greatest diversity of representations. (You'll see what I mean, later.)

Mr Great-Heart (GH): A Pastor-figure guide, chaperone, and bodyguard for the women, boys, and rag-tag group of aged and infirm who pilgrimage through Part II. He is handy with a sword and somewhat of a giant magnet. He can give theology lectures at the drop of a hat.

Gaius (GAI): Takes his name from the book of Acts (19:29; 20:4) and Romans (16:23) where he hosts the apostle Paul. In the Pilgrimverse, appropriately, he owns an inn and offers hospitality and conversation to pilgrims along the way in Part II. He is given to unsolicited match-making, and also has a daughter, Phebe, who comes in handy in that regard.

Introduction

Mnason (MNA): His name is also taken from the book of Acts (21:16); he lives in Vanity, and gathers a growing fellowship of believers around him, in Part II. He's big into church history and celebrating the role of women in the church. He also has a couple of daughters. He gets them married off, too.

Christiana (CNA): Doubts her husband in Part I, but is convicted to follow him in Part II. Mother of four boys, and "Naomi" to Mercy's "Ruth" throughout their joint pilgrimage.

Mercy (MER): Christiana's companion throughout the pilgrimage of Part II. Known for fainting with anxiety at the Wicket Gate, Mercy is generous to those in need, discerning of the faults of unsuitable male suitors, and sings for joy at the macabre hanging of pilgrims' opponents. She marries Matthew, becoming Christiana's daughter-in-law.

James (JAM): Youngest of four sons of Christian and Christiana, marries Phebe, and knows some solid basic theology.

Phebe (PHE): Daughter of Gaius, marries James, has a baby, and that is about all we know about Phebe in Part II.

Mr Worldly-Wiseman (W-W): Entices Christian to leave the narrow path to the Wicket Gate with the offer of an easier way to lose his burden. Doubts that Bible reading can do you any good but reckons a morally upstanding civic life will do the job of saving your soul. Often portrayed as an upper-class dandy with a taste for finer fashions of clothing.

Pliable (PLI): A neighbor of Christian's from the City of Destruction, who is flexible enough with his schedule to drop everything and join the pilgrimage to the Celestial City . . . until running into difficulty, at which he promptly gives up and slinks home, much to the amusement and mockery of his neighbors.

Shepherd boy (SB): Sings a song extolling humility in the here and now, with hope of eternal glory later. This is in the beautiful Valley of Humiliation in Part II. His song is briefly a hymn for the church in the nineteenth century. He is jealous of Valiant-for-truth whose words become a much more famous and enduring hymn in the Pilgrimverse.

Valiant-for-truth (VFT): A sturdy warrior in Part II who utters words of poetry that are much later set to music and so become a hymn for the church which echoes around the Pilgrimverse. Also known for his awesome double-edged sword.

Interpreter (INT): Loves displaying images and scenarios that illustrate spiritual truths while hosting and nurturing new converts in the way of Christian salvation. Often taken, by commentators and editors, to be a figure for the Holy Spirit.

Watchful (WAT): Along with Knowledge, Experience, and Sincere, he is one of the Shepherds of the Delectable Mountains. He loves instructing pilgrims and equipping them for their journey. His surrounding geography provides visual illustration for his teaching. He also has a telescope that gives a view of the Celestial City itself. (He is not the Watchful who serves as the Porter of the Palace Beautiful.)

Christian (CHR): Formerly known as Graceless, is convicted of his sin by Bible reading, gains a burden, and is pointed by Evangelist to the Wicket Gate, and on to the Celestial City. Losing his burden at the cross, Christian travels through trials and tribulations, some brought on by his own foolishness, until crossing the River of Death to reach his destination. (No spoiler, it's in Bunyan's book title.)

Ignorance (IGN): A young, self-confident chap, he ignores clear sound gospel teaching, preferring to think that his very excellent religious thoughts and efforts will be recognized as worthy and counted as righteous to secure him entry to the Celestial City. He crosses the river of death, but finds no admittance. The Pilgrimverse assigns him a variety of fates, but Bunyan is clear—he is carted off to hell.

Old Mr Honest (HON): In Part II, he is old and not just inclined to honesty, but simply honest in all his dealings—the emphasis on acts rather than virtue.

Mr Ready-to-halt (RTH): A slower pilgrim on account of using crutches to help him walk, in Part II. Mr Ready-to-halt takes his name from Ps 38:17 in the King James Version. Can be courageous and even breaks into dancing when Giant Despair is dispatched. Gets to leave his crutches behind when he is summoned to cross the River of Death to the Celestial City.

Introduction

Evangelist (EVA): Confronts Graceless/Christian with the gospel challenge to fly from the wrath to come and head to the Wicket Gate which gives entry to the straight and narrow path of salvation. He pops up to encourage and rebuke, as needed, in accompanying pilgrims in Part I.

A brief poem is offered below to start this book. This is an homage and imitation of John Bunyan's habit of prefacing his stories with explanatory verse. His poems, which are more exacting in their rhyme schemes than the one here, explain his motivations and goals for writing in the way that he did:

When I at first set fingers to keyboard
the book I had in mind was another,
a ponderous tome of dubious need,
a theology of the reception of *The Pilgrim's Progress*.

But my prose alongside John Bunyan's paled,
drowned in academese and footnoted asides.
What would this same examination look like
If set out, Pilgrim-style, and dialogue-wise?
Could this be a more faithful way to
capture the book's multiple afterlives?
From song and dance, to colorful images
in illustrations and comics, like a Marvel franchise.
A multiverse of alternative worlds
of Christian's journey is here recounted,
with tweaks, twist, and swirls
across too many genres to be counted.
What shall we call this? These material worlds of adventure?
The "Pilgrimverse" works, so I'll proceed without censure.

The idea of another voyage started to emerge,
Faithful and Hopeful might lead the charge:
Advancing over the terrain of reception
(meaning the history of how the book is received
rather than a post wedding party, or digital signal retention).
Instead of a Wicket Gate and one narrow way,
Portals lead into books, sights, sounds of their day.
When Bunyan's tale is less known than once it was,
and channeled through kids' books or Cliff notes online,
Faithful can ask how this came from that,

In what way can truth be adapted? And Hopeful
can counter that many are the ways a story can thrive
in God's economy until final judgment arrives?
Can the gospel bear fruit in adapted clothes
cut for this age? Can the Pilgrimverse widen or simply
corrupt? Is chaos the norm as each one does
as they see fit in their own eyes?
Or can a new packaging of Bunyan's tale
serve truth in casting out lies?
Faithful and Hopeful will be joined on the way
by Mr Researcher, and a cast of characters having their say.
Will you, Reader, cheer us and not wish us the worst,
as we set out to explore the Pilgrimverse?

As I wandered through the wilderness of the world wide web, my searches led me to a certain site, where I laid down my head to sleep. And as I slept, I dreamed a dream. I dreamed that I saw John Bunyan's famous book, *The Pilgrim's Progress*, laying open on a desk. And as I looked, I saw two men, as it were, detach themselves from their place in one or another of the book's illustrations, pull themselves out of the text block, clumsily bumping into each other to stand atop the book, its open pages below their feet, looking this way and that. Two-dimensional figures taking their bearings in three-dimensional space. Looking at each other, they let out a cry: "What shall we do?"

Upon hearing the other's voice, each looked around with shock. They had evidently emerged from a book copy that had never been read aloud. Their actual voices came as a surprising but joyful gift. And when the shock had passed, they turned to smiling, then chuckling, and then they all but fell about laughing. Now leaning on each other to avoid, so they feared, dissolving and tumbling back into the book's pages, were such a thing still possible, they gradually ran out of breath, and, burdened by their shared hilarity, bent down toward each other. They eventually pushed each other back up to standing straight.

"Well, that was unexpected!" said the older man, Faithful.

The younger, Hopeful, replied, "You can say that again. One minute, we're in the story, bound by Bunyan's pen, and now, we've escaped. Like Christian from captivity in Vanity, only wilder."

Introduction

Narrator (to the reader): There will be references to events in *The Pilgrim's Progress* Parts I and II throughout that will be more informative once you've read or recalled the book (or listened to the audiobook, watched the movie, etc.). I'll review the outline of the plot in a bit.

NAR (to Faithful): How do you think this has happened, Faithful?

FAI: I have no idea. You're sure you didn't have a hidden key on you to escape the book, Hopeful?

HOP: Like Christian in Doubting Castle? I wish! At least then I'd have some explanation . . .

    They trailed off chatting, to look around them some more. The desk, bookshelves around it, and the surrounding floor were all thick with The Pilgrim's Progress. At least, many, many book copies and book adaptations were in evidence, as well as CD cases, and DVDs, and board game boxes. *Pilgrim's Progress* artwork was displayed on what little wall or shelf opening was not filled with the other collectibles. At the center of the desk was a laptop computer, internet browser open to an equally overflowing bookmarks menu of *The Pilgrim's Progress* related sites and articles.

FAI: Are you recognizing what I'm recognizing? 'Cos if you're seeing DVDs, and web pages like I am, don't you think it's a little strange?

HOP: How so?

FAI: Well, how would I even know what any of those things are?

HOP: Or me, for that matter? What with our having been written up and published in the late seventeenth century, you mean? Yeah, I think that's a little odd.

    Both are stumped for a while, still standing on the pages of the book from which they've emerged. Then Faithful jumps from the book to the desktop, and beckons Hopeful to follow. At his indication, they both heave on the front book cover to slowly close the book. Faithful then jumps forward and opens just the first few pages until he comes upon the publication date: 2023.

FAI: That explains it, I suppose, we're from a modern reprint!

HOP: But that doesn't explain why we're not speaking Bunyan-style anymore. Although come to think of it, I'm not sure that style was ever allowed to totally settle.

NAR (to reader): We'll learn more about that in the first expedition in chapter 2.

Even dreaming, I was starting to feel a little awkward. I was conscious enough to know Faithful and Hopeful were speaking like me. Perhaps I oughtn't to pretend that I knew their minds so omnisciently, as the Narrator. Or rather, I should acknowledge to you, the reader, that my biases and preferences do really dictate how the characters respond and engage the adventures that are ahead. And while I have tried to be inclusive and respectful of the diversity of the Pilgrimverse, my actual non-omniscience as author-Narrator, the limitations of my knowledge, writing, and time for research placed limits on how much of the Pilgrimverse is explored and reported within these pages. Also, the irony of their breaking out of their book as a condition of being captured in mine caused me some discomfort, until I remembered they were always just allegorical characters in any case. Probably best to go full Bunyan on them and mostly fade out as a narrator, unless clear intervention is needed.

I saw that, (ok, it's harder to let go than I thought), as the two men looked about them, they were approached by a bespectacled, balding giant with a neatly trimmed, graying beard. His name was Researcher. On seeing him, the two cried out again, "What shall we do?" The giant leaned in, with apparent menace, as it is fairly easy to do as a giant, by definition, and "asked them whence they were, and what they did in his [Study]. They told him they were Pilgrims, and that they had lost their way. Then said the Giant, you have this night trespassed on me by trampling in and lying on my [Desk], and therefore you must go along with me."

FAI: Go where, exactly?

HOP: And haven't I heard that speech before somewhere?

RES (now smiling): I'm sorry about that. It's hard not to menace when you have the size advantage. It was petty of me. I'm actually not a giant. I'm just a regular human. And I'm friendly. I hate to break it you, but, well, it's you guys who are little. And, yes, Hopeful, you heard that from Giant Despair when you and Christian slept in his ground outside Doubting Castle. I was quoting, with a little adaptation. People do it all the time, you'll see!

HOP: I thought it felt a little close to the bone . . .

FAI: So, you say you're friendly, but then you scare my friend like that?

Introduction

RES: Can we start again?

HOP: What do you mean?

RES: With that question of yours.

FAI: You mean, What shall we do?

RES: Yes. I'm glad you asked, because I have a job for you both.

FAI: I'm sure that's very kind, but we're allegorical characters from a story, we just need help getting back whence we came.

HOP: Ooh, listen to you with your fancy "whence"! He means "where we came from."

RES: Thank you. You mean, like *The Wizard of Oz*, where Frank Baum famously borrows the whole dream sequence framing and then copies the detail about the Enchanted Ground from *The Pilgrim's Progress*?

HOP: We've not met a Wizard or a Frank.

RES: But you might!

FAI: How so? Look, I'm catching on fast, can't we just click our heels and return to our book.

RES: No, I need some help. You see I'm writing a book about how *The Pilgrim's Progress* has been adapted and received.

HOP: Why?

RES: Pardon?

FAI: He said, Why?

HOP: Yeah, you've got to have a reason. Why are you writing this book? 'Cos John Bunyan knew why he was writing his book.

FAI: That's right. He leaves his readers in no doubt that he wants to encourage them in their walk as Christians. And by walk I mean life, although most would probably walk as there were no cars, buses, trains, or planes back then.

HOP: What Faithful means is that Bunyan wanted the reader to "read thyself [and] know whether thou art blest or not, [by laying their] Book, th[eir] Head, and Heart together."

RES: OK, I see your point. Well, I guess I want to encourage people who come across *The Pilgrim's Progress* today in some form or other. I want to offer them perspectives on their encounters that will ask how faithful their experience was to what Bunyan wanted to deliver in his original text. I also want to ask what hope is embodied in their encounter with *The Pilgrim's Progress* that is a fruit of, or consistent with, or a new departure from, that original?

FAI: Did you hear him mention us both there, Hopeful?

HOP: I did. Did that strike you as suspicious?

FAI: Unlikely to have been a coincidence, is what I am thinking right now.

HOP: Admittedly these are strange moments we're living, but I'm of one mind with you on this one. Faithfulness I get, but hope? That's more of a head scratcher.

FAI: Surely faithfulness to the original is all that counts.

HOP: Well, I'm not sure that's the case. For starters, Bunyan would want us to be faithful to the gospel if we found that it critiqued his book, notwithstanding his godly intentions.

FAI: You're saying Bunyan could have been blinkered in some way to the truth that he wanted to witness to in his writing.

RES: That's it.

HOP: And the hope bit?

RES: That's why you two need to explore the Pilgrimverse together. Hope in a history of reception is going to have to point to developments, redeployments, and recontextualizations of the work in ways that magnify beauties, remedy deficiencies, or supplement and strengthen the encouragement to flourishing that the story holds out, as text or performance or product.

HOP and FAI: Huh?

RES: I'm going to employ you guys to explore the Pilgrimverse for me!

FAI: Ok, well fine, but could you please go easy on the long words.

RES: Sorry, it a professional hazard. I think you guys will keep this accessible as we chat and then you report back along the way through the Pilgrimverse.

NAR: And I'll help you frame things with some choice verses from the Bible, and then in summing things up every so often, Mr Researcher.

Introduction

RES: (Looking around him for the source of the voice from above) Right, well, thanks, um, Mr Narrator?

NAR: You're all most welcome.

RES: Anyway, like I said, I'm going to employ you guys to explore the Pilgrimverse for me.

FAI & HOP: Hold on, though! The what, now?!

RES: The Pilgrimverse. I made it up. Didn't you see the Apology? At the top here?

HOP: This is getting a bit too meta, but no, no one actually reads poetic intros if there's regular prose beneath it. How many people do you think read Bunyan's Author's Apology?

RES: OK, point taken. But they should, you know. Still: the Pilgrimverse. Actually, I think it's a workable term for the phenomena of *The Pilgrim's Progress* reception. First, books come in all kinds of shapes and sizes, and editions, and target readerships, and then adaptations, abridgements, and translations. That's a whole world in itself, but The Pilgrim's Progress is so much more than a book now. Artists have turned it into comics and graphic novels and pop-up books. It's been made into board games, a video game, and table theater toys. It's been animated on film, as well as recreated on the stage, as a play, as musical theater, ballet, breakdance, and opera. Other sounds enliven audiobooks and voice dramatizations. There's even a marionette performance.

HOP: Wow, that's a lot.

RES: I've not finished. *The Pilgrim's Progress* is used to support marriage counseling, and parenting, homeschooling, and afterschool clubs for urban youth. Leisure and business, hobbies and crafts all get caught up in the Pilgrimverse.

FAI: Is that it?

RES: There are probably things I've forgotten. Oh, yes, like Magic Lantern slides and retreat center statues and jazz recordings.

HOP: All right, we get the picture. How exactly do we help?

RES: Well, I have a map.

With that Researcher handed over a tiny scroll on which the two men could see a schematic map of the desk they were standing on. After looking at the map a while, they both look back up at the giant human. They observed that the map seemed to show a route around and over the various piles and devices on the desk without much indication of what would be found.

FAI (hopefully): Looks like a little stroll?

HOP (doubtfully): That big pile looks a bit rickety to me.

RES: You're still narrative characters, so I can promise you that you won't come to any harm. But the journey looks deceptively short. You see, on this journey, there is no single Wicket Gate. It's not a salvation journey but more of a salvaging journey, if you will. Each pile of materials or device on the desk has a portal into the interior world of the Pilgrimverse. It was through one of them that you got out here. There could well be by-ways that I don't know how to map yet.

HOP: A By-way is just a fancy, old fashioned, John Bunyan term for a path or road, right?

RES: Again, sorry about that. Yes. Bunyan-speak can be hard to shake. So, anyway, you will both locate the portal for each section of the desk as mapped out here and allow yourselves to be transported into the Pilgrimverse. I'll then meet you after your survey to get your sense of what you've found.

FAI: And what then?

RES: Handily, the Narrator voice chap will be recording our conversation and is then going to incorporate the transcript of the expedition report into a book about the Pilgrimverse.

FAI: So each pile of Pilgrimverse products will be a chapter?

RES: More or less, yes.

HOP: That's quite a mountainous range of piles to climb.

RES: Maybe we could get a few other characters involved, if you think that would help?

    I saw in my dream that Faithful and Hopeful both replied at the same time to the effect that they would love others to help the survey. Then, I, the dreaming narrator, asked Researcher a question. (This is, admittedly, even for John Bunyan, an unusual move: he uses it to get information from Help about the Slough of Despond, in Part I, or to interact with Mr

Introduction

Sagacity at the beginning of Part II. It's basically a way within this dream construct to wrap up the book introduction in a satisfactory manner).

NAR: What else do readers need to know to orient themselves to what follows in this book?

RES: Well, it would definitely help to have a quick overview of the narrative contents of both Parts I and II.

NAR: I'm not at all surprised at your suggestions. Thanks for the prompt. So I'll now quickly summarize both books, and then . . .

FAI: Excuse me? What are we to do while you're doing this?

HOP: Yeah, we already know the plot 'cos we come from the book.

NAR: Of course! You guys can go off and prepare for your journey. I'll dream you back here when you're needed.

And in my dream, I see Faithful and Hopeful walk off. They make their way around an intimidatingly high pile of books in conversation with one another, something they'd never before done in such relaxed circumstances, as the reader will soon see.

NAR: So Part I of *The Pilgrim's Progress* begins with that Author's Apology we've already heard a little about. Readers can find it a bit off putting as a way into the book, a good number skipping it to where the story proper begins with famous lines: "As I wandered through the wilderness of this world." That's the opening I riffed off at the beginning of this introduction. What Bunyan's dreaming narrator sees is a man in rags, alone, bearing a heavy burden on his back, and holding a book, crying out "What shall I do?" We don't learn his name until quite a lot later in the text. He's simply the man. Like an everyman figure. His wife and boys don't buy the warning of imminent destruction by heavenly fire that he says his book speaks of. They mock and ignore him. He feels worse and worse and takes to wandering the fields reading his book and lamenting his condition. That's when Evangelist appears. He tells the man to "Fly from the wrath to come" and go to the Wicket Gate. It's not a WickeD gate! But the name is odd. It refers to a small pedestrian gate within a much larger set of gates or doors that would secure a town or city. (Think the gate to Bree in the Lord of the Rings movies.) In this case the Wicket Gate guards access to the King's highway, the narrow way of salvation, that leads to the Celestial City. Before he can reach it, the man must abandon his family and shake off the pursuit of two of his neighbors, Obstinate and Pliable.

He nearly doesn't reach the gate at all because of a couple of obstacles. First, he falls, with Pliable, into the Slough of Despond (meaning Despair). Helped out by, yes, Help, he then runs into Mr Worldly-Wiseman who tells him of a shortcut to remove his burden, by Mr Legality and his son Mr Civility in the town of Morality. It's in this dialogue we learn the burdened man is called Christian. We also have confirmed that the book he is reading is the Bible. Christian leaves the narrow path to take his advice but is brought back to the path by Evangelist after a run in with the law (biblical, not the police). Knocking at the Wicket Gate he is pulled in by the Porter, who sends him on to the House of the Interpreter. There he is instructed about grace and perseverance by a series of "emblems" or pictured scenarios. Only then is he sent on to experience the assurance of his salvation at the foot of a cross atop a hill where his burden falls from his back. Met by three shining ones there, he is promised forgiveness of his sins, given a new coat and a scroll which will function as a certificate to secure his entry to the Celestial City. Journeying onwards he comes to a steep hill and carelessly falls asleep in a shelter half-way up, losing his scroll in the process of waking and rushing upward to avoid nightfall. His hurry backfires, he returns and does find his scroll, but now is benighted (has to travel in the dark). Even so, he reaches the Palace Beautiful, having had his faith tested by two Lions guarding its approach. Here he receives churchly fellowship in the persons of four sisters, Discretion, Prudence, Patience, and Charity. He gives his testimony and here we learn that his name was formerly Graceless. He is given food and rest, and then equipped with armor for the next phase of his journey into the Valley of Humiliation. There he fights a monster called Apollyon whose devilish fiery darts are ultimately overcome by the sword of the Spirit as Christian calls out Scripture verses of gospel confidence. Even so, he must still then walk through the Valley of the Shadow of Death, again, by night, and face inner turmoil as fiends and foul goblins afflict him. He makes it through with prayer (a sword is no use) and the hope of catching up with a figure ahead of him on the path. He turns out to be a fellow townsman of the City of Destruction, Faithful. Christian and Faithful hear each other's stories of conversion and spiritual struggle. They also form a class double act in dealing with Talkative, who, when it comes to religion, is, naturally, all talk. Warned of danger ahead by the reappearing Evangelist, Christian and Faithful enter the town of Vanity, at whose Fair they refuse to buy anything. For their disruption of local custom, they

Introduction

are beaten, imprisoned, and at a rigged trial, Faithful is condemned to a gruesome death, and burned at the stake. (Happily, in death he is whisked off to heaven by a chariot of fire). Christian, meanwhile, miraculously escapes his arrest, and soon meets Hopeful who has been brought to faith by Faithful's witness. These two now travel together, doing dialogue battle with two-faced Mr By-Ends and his three friends, and avoiding the snares of Demas and Hill Lucre, until Christian leads them out of the way for a bit of meadow grass comfort for his feet. They end up sleeping the night on the lands of Giant Despair. He captures and imprisons them in his Doubting Castle and wills them to die. Another miraculous escape sees the two reach the Delectable Mountains, another churchly moment, where Shepherds give them their first blurry glimpse of the Celestial City. Setting off on the last leg of their journey, they run into a young man called Ignorance, whose confidence in his own works for acceptance at the heavenly city shapes the rest of the book. Despite warnings, the two pilgrims still fall victim to the Flatterer and captivity in his net. They have to be saved, and chastised, by another Shining One. They resist dissuasion to continue from Atheist, and make it through the bewitching Enchanted Ground by sharing Hopeful's story of conversion centered around justification by grace through faith in Jesus Christ. Christian even tells the story of Little Faith who manages the journey, barely, despite his little faith, on that same basis of justification. So, the next long dialogue with Ignorance, exposing his false confidence in his own satisfaction of God's demands is the bookend of Bunyan's main theological emphasis on grace that has run throughout. The pilgrims reach the borders of the Celestial City at Beulah Land to face the River of Death, which they must cross over to reach their destination. They do, not without drama, and are ushered beyond Bunyan's dreamer's sight into the City, just as the narrator also sees Ignorance turned away and cast into Hell.

I looked around for a helpful intervention from Researcher so that I could catch my breath, but he was just stood there smiling encouragingly, and I also realized I didn't need to catch my breath in a dream. So I plunged into Part II:

NAR: Another poem precedes the story of Part II. Here Bunyan defends his Part I as successful but also grievously pirated by cheap copycats since its original publication. He previews the characters of the story to come and suggests that Part II is the key by which to unpack Part I. We might think of it as overlaying not only the geography and itinerary of Part I but also its theology. Getting a little too elaborate, this Part begins with a dreaming narrator meeting another narrator, Mr Sagacity, who starts to tell the former what has happened to Christiana since Christian's adventure of Part I. (Mercifully, this double narration soon peters out, poor Mr Sagacity.) Christiana has a frightening dream that convicts her of her hard-heartedness toward her husband's faith. She then receives a heavenly visitor named Secret from whom she receives a letter of invitation to the Celestial City. Her neighbor's mockery notwithstanding, she gathers her four sons, and allows a younger neighbor Mercy to tag along, and sets out on pilgrimage. Using the stepping-stones that Christian had missed, they cross the Slough of Despond with ease, reaching the Wicket Gate quickly. Here Christiana knocks and gains entrance, while Mercy faints in anxiety that she has not received a proper call to salvation. She is admitted and they journey on. The two women attract the attention of violent men who would rape them, but escape through the arrival of Reliever, a man sent to save them when their cries were heard. They are to blame for their misfortune because they should have known they needed a guide. Reliever gets them to the Interpreter's House where they see what Christian saw and more, and the boys are tested on their knowledge of core Christian teaching at Palace Beautiful. With much giant killing, the party moves on and grows incrementally. The geography is the same but encountered on different terms. They see markers of Christian's earlier adventure. They add rescued or weak pilgrims to their number and thus pause at length at Gaius's Inn and then Mnason's house in Vanity. They defeat Giant Despair and destroy Doubting Castle and rescue more pilgrims. Eventually a very full party reaches Beulah Land, and some are called individually to cross the River of Death to the Celestial City, while the rest remain to further the life of the church as they await their call.

RES: That was quite a marathon, but you covered a lot of ground.

NAR: Thanks. There's a lot of delightful detail missing, but it can serve as a reminder to those who've read both parts.

RES: Or a prompt to finish reading for those who now remember that they never got around to finishing or even reading the real thing after early exposure to an adaptation.

NAR: Before I wake up from this introduction, I need to ask you to tell us about the map you gave Faithful and Hopeful just now.

Introduction

RES: Fine. Well, the first dimension of the Pilgrimverse to tackle is that of *The Pilgrim's Progress* as a text and a book, and the variety of what that entails.

And I saw ahead in my dream that, rather than Faithful and Hopeful, that bit of exploration would be done by Mr Great-Heart with Gaius and Mnason, but Researcher didn't know that, and I saw no reason to tell him. I like mixing it up a bit, socially.

RES: Next, we'll jump across to a graphic novel part of the Pilgrimverse.

I saw that Faithful and Hopeful would, in fact, be exploring this dimension. This and the following expedition would be the ones most densely framed by some history and theology. FYI, I say this in case readers are looking for greater levity, which emerges from the Home expedition onwards.

RES: Then, after that, I want us to explore the dimension that involves Bunyan's classic as an object of Christian devotional and Bible study, as well as its use in missionary evangelism.

This part of the Pilgrimverse journey would be undertaken by Christiana and Mercy.

RES: From this ministry context we switch focus to think of the Pilgrimverse as manifest in the book's impact on the home front of domestic family situations of marriage, parenting, and play, as well as its interaction with work and hobbies. This takes in children's adaptations to board games, advice manuals, and computer games.

I saw that James and Phebe (Christian and Christiana's son and Mnason's daughter—they didn't even make the summary above! Sorry) would lead this climb.

RES: From textual and visual material we turn then to discover the sounds of the Pilgrimverse, from audiobook to a whole range of musical productions, from opera, to prog rock, to jazz.

The Shepherd boy and Mr Valiant-for-Truth would lead this foray.

RES: Another way of seeing the sights of the Pilgrimverse turns us back to illustrations, monuments, plays, dance, and moving pictures of various forms, from animation to CGI and live action movies.

This, I saw, would be an expedition led by the Interpreter and the Shepherd, Watchful.

RES: And because so much of this Pilgrimverse is driven by creators enthusiastic about the book from an evangelical perspective, we'll include an exploration of the Pilgrimverse's margins. We'll showcase revisionary treatments that learn from the book at a different angle from the dominant one.

I saw that, no I won't tell you, you can wait to find out who would helm that expedition.

And then in my dream, I turned to Researcher to thank him, saying:

NAR: Thank you, Mr Researcher, I hope you find some useful material in all these dimensions of the Pilgrimverse.

I could see already that Researcher would be there at the conclusion to draw threads together, but my dreaming foresight (for the sake of suspense) couldn't yet discern who would help him. Would Christian make an appearance, or some Shining Ones? We'll be asking one last time the driving questions of what faithfulness and hope look like in the Pilgrimverse. What is the place of this story, text, book, or product in the lives of Christians and others at the present time? What are the responsibilities of contemporary reception? What prayers should accompany the expansion or contraction of the Pilgrimverse in years to come?

All told, as I started to awaken, my last thoughts were that this odyssey into the Pilgrimverse would be both a critique and a celebration. And it would be an invitation for others to join in and learn together.

In Hebrews, it is by faith that the universe is discerned as God's creation based on saving knowledge of Jesus Christ who redeems all things. As the verse at the beginning of this chapter states, what is visible was made out of nothing, but by God's word alone. The Pilgrimverse is not the universe, not even remotely. It is just a conceptual label for a host of ways of receiving one single book. Yet, in God's grace and provision, John Bunyan's book has had a considerable influence, and a respectable longevity in the church for the world and well beyond the church. It is a work, like all human work, made out of what is visible. It is not divine revelation, although it purports to lean very heavily on the Bible. Whatever Bunyan's suggestion of his spiritual inspiration in writing, his images and story mechanisms draw on prior learning and a cultural imagination. Certainly, he is shaped by his cultural, sociopolitical, and spiritual context, as those who have received his book have been by theirs. His chief authority, he would say, and his text testifies to this amply, is the Bible. Many who love the Bible have loved *The Pilgrim's Progress*. This

Introduction

Narrator prays that those who read further into this exploration of the Pilgrimverse will be encouraged that such a submission to Scripture still has life, even where death lurks to destroy, and that a work so imagined can fire up a critical discernment of Christian calling. Similarly, where critique is apposite in this Pilgrimverse, it is my prayer that the kind of confidence in what we cannot yet see, as the fulfillment of all things in Christ, allows us to soberly and cheerfully receive rebuke and correction in the journey.

Some readers will want to dig deeper. Each chapter ends with a list of Pilgrimverse products referred to, and sometimes a few extra items of suggested further reading. Much academic study of *The Pilgrim's* Progress, and John Bunyan's wider work, is hidden from the general reader in institutional libraries or behind subscription paywalls or in out of print or expensive books. That's part of the reason to explore the Pilgrimverse here, without footnotes or high level theorizing.

Now, before I awaken from this dream, I'll take you back to Mr Researcher's desk so that you are in a good position to observe how the journey into the Pilgrimverse begins. Enjoy!

Pilgrimverse Resources that connect with the overall goals of the expedition reports:

Bunyan Studies: A Journal of Reformation and Nonconformist Culture. https://johnbunyansociety.org/bunyan-studies-a-journal-of-reformation-and-nonconformist-culture/.

Davies, M., and W. R. Owens, eds. *The Oxford Handbook of John Bunyan.* Oxford: Oxford University Press, 2018.

Dunan-Page, Anne. *The Cambridge Companion to Bunyan.* Cambridge: Cambridge University Press, 2010.

Hofmeyr, Isabel. *The Portable Bunyan: A Transnational History of "The Pilgrim's Progress."* Princeton: Princeton University Press, 2004.

Horner, Barry E. *Pilgrim's Progress: Themes and Issues.* Auburn, MA: Evangelical, 2003.

Milne, Kirsty. *At Vanity Fair: From Bunyan to Thackeray.* Cambridge: Cambridge University Press, 2015.

Owens, W. R., and S. Sim, eds. *Reception, Appropriation, Recollection: Bunyan's Pilgrim's Progress.* Religions and Discourse 33. Bern, Switzerland: Peter Lang, 2007.

"Professor Pilgrim's Progress: Teaching a Spiritual Classic in a Selfie World." https://www.professorpilgrimsprogress.com/.

The Recorder. Newsletter of the International John Bunyan Society. https://johnbunyansociety.org/the-newsletter/.

2

Books

> The Lord detests dishonest scales,
> but accurate weights find favor with him.
>
> PROVERBS 11:1

RES: Where are the explorers when you need them?

I saw in my dream that Researcher was standing by his desk with its piles of Pilgrimverse products, looking in vain for Faithful and Hopeful. He was expecting them to continue on the journey he had told them about in the introduction. In fact, the task ahead was possibly the most physically demanding: the pile of book copies of *The Pilgrim's Progress* was dauntingly high. Still, Faithful must have navigated the same Hill Difficulty that Christian had struggled to overcome, so his training for the challenge was not in doubt. Hopeful's credentials must have been the same, technically, given that he too gained entrance to the Celestial City so must have come through the Wicket Gate, by way of the Cross, even though his journey seems to have begun in Vanity under the influence of Faithful's evangelistic witness. I recalled in my dream that some held that the City of Destruction and Vanity were effectively the same location in regard to their worldliness and opposition to the truth of the gospel. Quickly setting such brain teasers aside, I looked to see how the Researcher would proceed.

RES: Anyone going to help me?

    I saw that a group of three characters emerged from behind the stack of books and made their way to the center of the desk in response to Researcher's cry.

Great-Heart: We will help you. What is your charge?

RES: Oh, you don't need to pay me anything, although I do hope you'll help me for free. Grants in the humanities are hard to come by . . .

GH: You misunderstand me, Giant. By "charge," I meant "commission" or "challenge" or even "task" for us to perform?

RES: Oh, so sorry. I should have figured your speech might be a little formal. Your armor is quite commanding, if I might say so?

GH: I'm not one to dress down.

RES: Quite. You're Great-Heart, aren't you?

GH: I am, and may I also present to you my two companions, Gaius and Mnason.

RES: Pleased to meet you. Let me reassure you, and myself, just so we're clear: I'm not a giant, just an ordinary sized human, ok?

Gaius: Fine by me.

Mnason: I do my best to live at peace with all.

GH: I admit to getting a bit sword-happy around Giants, but you know that I know that I could dispatch you if you were to act up, so we can certainly maintain a truce.

    I recalled in my dream that Great-Heart had killed more than a few different giants and monsters in PP Part II, even with the help of Mnason at one point. Gaius, however, was more known for his hospitality to fellow-pilgrims than for his hospitalizing of enemies.

RES: Well, thanks, I think. That awkwardness dealt with, here's the charge: I want you guys to explore different book editions of the Pilgrimverse.

GAI: All of them?

RES: Well, no. Just a sample. Give me a sense of the scope through time, and then the variety. I can't prejudge what you'll find, but I reckon there's going to be commonality and variety.

GH: It's a good job there are three of us. We'll divide and conquer after an initial reccy.

GAI: We don't have to wreck things, do we?

MNA: That's just his soldier speak for sussing things out, getting the lie of the land, as it were.

GH: Reconnoitering, from the French. Which will be handy as I see a few French translations ahead.

RES: Best of luck! I'll meet you back here later. Oh, try to stick, first, to full texts and then, if you have time, you can survey some abridgements and adaptations, but don't worry about those intended for children, for now. And don't worry about the illustrations, either—we'll circle back round to those later.

The Researcher turned away and left the office while Great-Heart complained to his companions that having to count on luck would mean they were not trusting in God's sovereign providence. Telling the soldier to lighten up, the three set off, Great-Heart in the lead, Mnason following, and Gaius taking up the rear, carrying a bag of provisions in case of snack breaks. I heard him muttering that he should have brought more liquid as the journey ahead looked decidedly dry.

The climb to the top of this particular pile of books was difficult. It was certainly made harder by the crumbling of bindings up to two hundred years old, rendering foot and hand holds precarious. But they tackled it efficiently, with the added benefit of being two-dimensional figures which meant they carried a lot less weight than had they been filled out. I knew these were the best characters for the task because of the roles they each assumed in Part II, interpreting and explaining Christian's earlier journey and the theology undergirding it to those they interacted with. Also, it happened that Part II as a text hadn't gone through much change at the hands of author and publisher in early printings which, they were about to find, was not true of Part I.

They came to the top of the pile and saw by a shimmering light that the portal into this dimension of the Pilgrimverse was the front cover illustration of Evangelist pointing Christian toward the wicket gate on the Moody Colportage Library edition from the early 1900s.

GAI: Before we dive in, I want to make an observation about the external geography of this area of the Pilgrimverse.

MNA: Go on.

GAI: If all these books we have been scrambling over are but a sample of hundreds and hundreds of editions of *The Pilgrim's Progress*, we have to recognize what a variety of physical items we're encountering.

GH: He's right. There are elaborately embossed hard back volumes with gilt edged pages, and then there are flimsy paperback tracts.

MNA: Some books include us, that is, Part II, while others don't.

GAI: From oversized heavy collectors editions to tightly bound, thin volumes with the flimsiest of paper, the thickness of the books varies as well as the height.

MNA: Some of these books will have been expensive, designed for collectors, with small print runs. That Folio edition is one of 750. But it's far too big for even a Giant to actually hold in their lap to read comfortably.

GH: And not cheap. But the tract editions are cheap and cheerful. This is a book that appeals to, or is produced to distribute to, a wide range of readers.

GAI: And readers know that their experience in reading is affected by the physicality of the book—even including the device on which they might download a digital text.

MNA: Look at you, all fancy and modern!

GH: He's right, again. Also, the publisher's brand confers identity on a book, as a religious or trade press product, as part of an academic series or prestigious book collectors' edition.

    They paused to marvel once more at the diversity of the many book copies over which they had climbed to reach the summit. But the portal into the fullness of this area of the Pilgrimverse still beckoned. Gently lifting up the picture from the book cover with the tip of his sword, in view of the flimsy nature of this old book copy, Great-Heart bid the other two follow him as he launched himself through the portal. Gaius and Mnason were glad he had gone first but followed quickly after him. Their journey took them over the printed words of book copies representing the span of the nearly 350 year published history of the work. Tasked to leave consideration of the illustrations until later, they were concentrating on the text, or as it turned out, the texts. Having gathered information, they each made their way back to the portal and clambered out to the book mountain peak, Great-Heart struggling the most on account of his armor.

GH: (Catching his breath) All right, gentlemen. Let's rest here a minute until Researcher arrives and then we'll debrief our collected intel.

MNA: Gaius, let's have those snacks.

So they sat around munching on snacks, happy to rest in silence as they collected their thoughts on the textual journey they'd been on. After a while, Researcher entered the office and approached the desk, asking for their findings.

GAI: I have to say, I was actually most surprised by the uneven and shifting footing as I crossed the terrain of this dimension.

MNA: Me, too! I have to say that over in Part II we have it a little gentler, text-wise.

GH: I'm glad to have made it through the modern English language zone . . .

GAI: . . . and the foreign language section was enormous, I only surveyed a small portion, I'm afraid.

RES: There's only so much we can navigate of this Pilgrimverse. Tell me about the your discoveries.

MNA: It turns out that most people refer to Part I as *The Pilgrim's Progress*. Our Part II is not so hot a commodity, it seems. But then, what's even more interesting is that Part I rarely stays the same.

RES: How so?

MNA: Well, Bunyan had written it mostly, so far as we know, from prison—his dreaming narrator refers to a Den, spelled D-E-N-N, in the opening lines of the narrative.

GH: And then, in the 3rd edition and following, that is, from 1679, Bunyan supplies a marginal note to indicate that the Den is "The Gaol."

GAI: Which by the 11th edition of 1688, the year the author died, Den has lost its extra "n" at the end, and the spelling of "Gaol" has changed to the more modern English, "Jail."

MNA: Not to mention the typos in some early editions that spell "Gaol" as "Goal!" So, it turns out that the Part I runs through eleven editions in Bunyan's lifetime and clever scholars can actually track the connections between these editions in terms of errors that persist between them, for example.

GH: And not only are there details that differ, so that many of the biblical references included by Bunyan are added in the second and third editions, but also major sections of the story as known in the twenty-first century are not in the first edition of 1678.

MNA: That's right. There is no Mr Worldly-Wiseman, nor are there the second and third meetings with Evangelist that normally occur after the encounter with Mr Worldly-Wiseman and before the adventure in Vanity Fair; there's no By-Ends and his three friends; no Giant Despair's wife. All these elements are added for the second edition, except for By-Ends who only appears in the third edition. Certainly, these are from Bunyan's pen. All of which is to say that the story most often referred to as *The Pilgrim's Progress* is not entirely that of the first edition alone.

GAI: And I think you'll want to come back to this for the exploration of the Pilgrimverse to families and children, but the first edition just has Christian running away after his meeting with Evangelist, abandoning his wife and children as they call after him, without ever having shared his burden with them. And this silence affects the dialogues he has later at Palace Beautiful. Bunyan only include the man's interactions with his family before his departure from the second edition.

RES: So what you're saying is that, for those who would think the first edition is the best representation of the text that Bunyan intended, it turns out to be lacking.

MNA: That's exactly it. So much so, that when publishers in the nineteenth and twentieth century produce facsimiles of the first edition they still include the second and third edition additions as integral to the "real text"!

RES: Even though readers of the first edition would never have seen the book copy the facsimile's claim to reproduce!

GAI: Right. And we can see that Bunyan, or his publisher printer, 'cos it's impossible to tell who exactly is making these changes, starts tidying up spelling and grammar through those eleven editions.

GH: It seems that the working relationship of author and printer could mean that any changes in Bunyan's lifetime, particularly of adding text or notes, would have been from the author, but that changes in spellings, cutting redundant repetition that might have affected spacing of the type on a page, and the most obvious trackable typographical errors could have happened independently of Bunyan's explicit input.

RES: I've come across these phenomena in preparing an edition of *The Pilgrim's Progress*. My co-editor and I needed to make the text accessible to contemporary undergraduate readers while keeping a seventeenth-century, Bunyan flavor. We actually drew on the 11th edition of the text which Roger Pooley prepared for the Penguin Classics edition, and then compared with the texts prepared by W. R. Owens for the Oxford World's Classics and the authoritative text prepared by Roger Sharrock for the second Clarendon Press, Oxford edition of 1960.

MNA: And those are some big-hitting Bunyan scholar names, right there!

RES: We found that the eleventh edition sometimes elided small portions of the first and third editions' text. The smoothing of grammar and spelling was often an improvement but the text still required us to intervene for readability today. Sometimes just shortening very long sentences was the best move, at other times we slightly altered word order, and updated spellings to American usage for our publisher.

GH: Well, it turns out, whether acknowledged or not, this happens a lot with the book. Even editions that do not advertise that they are modernizing the English often make all sorts of interventions to tidy things up for their readers.

MNA: So, a deluxe edition printed in 2023, refers to its source text as a manuscript of *The Pilgrim's Progress* by John Bunyan that was published in 1678. Yet, the printed text of this edition is a modernized version, immediately apparent in reading the famous opening paragraphs.

RES: And is this a problem, do we think?

MNA: Not, so it seems, for one reader, at least. A certain C. Braun leaves a review on Amazon.com, writing, "The Pilgrim's Progress is a classic for a reason. This version is ever so slightly adapted with more modern English. The actual book makes no mention of who is responsible for the editing, but I really enjoyed this version and it's very close to the original, with better punctuation."

GAI: It does, at least, get at the question of what the book is: is it the message conveyed in the most readable form of the story, or the "original," Bunyan-authored text. It must be said that the further from the authorizing text of those early editions in interpretative modernizing the closer an edition comes to an adaptation.

GH: And the adaptations of the book are not just to do with the main text. Think about the visual impact of Bunyan's marginal notes and references.

RES: What do you notice happens to these?

MNA: Well, they promote what some scholars call intensive and discontinuous reading. The reader's eye is drawn out of the story to the guiding narrative of the author who highlights in summary key movements of the text.

GAI: Somewhat erratically, it has to be said.

MNA: But also, sometimes to creative and even comic effect. At Vanity Fair, the beautifully onomatopoeic word "Hubbub" describes the commotion caused by Christian and Faithful when they refuse to buy anything but the truth. So, Bunyan adds to his margins a constant shout out to the hubbub: "The Fair in a hubbub about them," "The first cause of the hubbub," "The second cause of the hubbub," "Third cause of the hubbub," and lastly, "The Fair in a hubbub." He compounds the narrative drama with this insistent refrain. This humorous repetition is then offset by the increasingly menacing notes that accompany the pilgrim's imprisonment, and trial, and condemnation, culminating with "The cruel death of Faithful."

GAI: Only to then be relieved by the story that accompanies the note, "A Chariot and Horses wait to take away Faithful."

GH: That's also a good point. Many times Bunyan will quote from or allude to the Bible but it doesn't mean that he will give a marginal reference. So here, the reader is supposed to recall the biblical story of Elijah the prophet being carried up to heaven by a chariot and horses of fire in 2 Kings 2:11. But Bunyan doesn't give the reference.

RES: Why not, do you think?

GH: I suspect it is a combination of his being deeply familiar with the Bible so that he is not looking up all these references and allusions as he writes, as well as a confidence that his readers would have equal command of the biblical text so that the references just aren't always necessary.

MNA: Another example of those fun notes, although more macabre, are the chronicling of the days Christian and Hopeful are held in Giant Despair's Doubting Castle.

GAI: The text says "Here they lay from Wednesday Morning till Saturday Night."

MNA: And then the marginal notes capture the transition of days, "On Thursday Giant Despair beats his Prisoners," "On Friday, Giant Despair counsels them to kill themselves" . . .

GAI: And then a little light relief: "The Giant sometimes has fits" . . .

MNA: Till we get to "On Saturday the Giant threatened that shortly he would pull them to pieces."

GH: And the very next marginal note is to "A Key in Christian's bosom called Promise, opens any Lock in Doubting Castle." That's to say, Bunyan is making very obvious to his readers that he intends them to notice that Sunday is the day of promise, the day of the clinging to the promises of God, which is a real encouragement to his Christian readers, who are brought low in their private lives during the week by doubt and despair, to look forward to the release of the ministry of the word in their church worship gathering. Even the fact that the two prisoners began to pray on Saturday about midnight is an allusion to Acts 16:25 when Paul and Silas are also praying about midnight and find themselves miraculously released from captivity. And again, here, Bunyan doesn't give his biblical reference in the margin.

GAI: And what we notice happening with later editions of the book is that it is most likely that the marginal notes, those ones that guide and point to interpretation of the text, even if, or maybe because they seem just to re-narrate events, well, these are the most likely to get cut.

MNA: It seems that whatever the technological affordances of seventeenth-century printing were, later publishers are more reluctant to generate marginal text alongside the main text.

GH: This means that Bible references often get set into the narrative text in parentheses. Which works if it is very clear what Bunyan's intends to connect his biblical reference to, a choice phrase or actual quote from Scripture, say.

MN: Not so well, if he seems to be amassing proof texts for his overall sensibility without having an exact textual hanging point—like when he piles up references to the last things for the man with the nightmare at the end of the Interpreter's House visit in Part I, not all of which support a clear element of the text.

GA: And then, some editions, instead of drawing their readers from the text interruptively with a biblical reference, have more recently decided to insert the full wording of the Bible reference. Sometimes this is in the body of the text, which then makes the reading a lot heavier and confused, the opposite of the actually fairly clear way in which Bunyan writes. Or the Bible references remain in the margins with the text added. The most recent version of this was only partially successful for two reasons: first, with too many references only some could have their full text added for space considerations—and then you have the bias of an editor deciding which verses to give preferential quotation treatment (possibly retrospectively imposing that weighting back on Bunyan as author.) Second, the Bible references work best, as I see it, when they are closest in language to Bunyan's own, which means the wording should be from the King James Version. Once you put the words in and they're from a more modern version the resonance to Bunyan's writing is less accurate.

GH: It's the challenge of really working with two books as you read in the Pilgrimverse, Bunyan's text and Bunyan's Bible.

RES: So do you reckon that one way of meeting that challenge would be to alter the wording of Bunyan's quotations and allusions to fit one contemporary English Bible translation? So we'd have the modernized English, NIV edition of *The Pilgrim's Progress*, or the ESV, or CSB, New Living, or even The Message versions?

GH: There'd probably be a market for that kind of tie-in. It's truly remarkable how many editions of this books there have been.

RES: So let me summarize, you've noticed that the text is a little unstable, given that we only have copies of editions rather than any original manuscript. But so far we've been talking about Part I. What about Part II?

MNA: That's our neck of the words, storyline-wise. And the fact is, it doesn't seem to capture the imagination quite like Part I does.

GAI: There is a second edition after the 1684 first publication. That's in 1686 with another printing in 1687. And there are Scripture references and marginal notes that are added, but the narrative text remains steady apart from some tidying of spelling and grammar, like with Part I.

MNA: For a while the books are published separately, but by the nineteenth century onwards both Parts can be published together.

GH: And don't forget Part III!

GAI and MNA: (together) No! We said we wouldn't mention it!

RES: It's OK. I know about it already. You're right, many readers of *The Pilgrim's Progress* in the seventeenth and eighteenth centuries may have found themselves enjoying 3 parts of the story. The Part III collated with I and II is one published in 1693 after Bunyan had died in 1688. It follows *Tender-conscience* on a journey that struggles to emulate Bunyan's theological confidence in Reformation justification by grace through faith. Instead, NOT-Bunyan offers a moralistic journey of self-discipline, but this didn't stop publishers, even once identified as false, from bundling the now recognized as illegitimate successor with the first two parts. But once a more elite readership started paying scholarly attention to Bunyan's book the fake third part starts to fade from the scene.

MNA: Are you saying the readership changes over time?

RES: Yes. Look, the first book copies of *The Pilgrim's Progress* were, compared to the standard modern paperback, tiny. And they would be dwarfed by the commemorative hardbacks that scatter the market today. I've held in my hand some of these early editions at the Huntington Library, in San Marino, California. They would have been undistinguished to look at. A text-filled title page cheaply binding the rest of the book. Not any different, certainly, from other books at a time when publishing is exploding, and particularly with religious argument coming from and aimed at an unusually wide spectrum of society. Readership is growing with advances in literacy brought about by a combination of Protestant religiosity, civic opportunity, and social disruption affording some degree of mobility for the poorer person. Bunyan, as an uneducated writer of the middling, artisan class, was not alone. But, ironically, in the research collection of the Huntington, these cheap early editions of *The Pilgrim's Progress* are now ornately gilt-edged and bound in red Morocco-leather hardback covers, kept even safer within custom-made and tightly fitting book size boxes. The cheap has become, by rarity, age, and collector zeal, ornamented, protected, and pricey. Of course, it is the very fragility of cheap originals that ensures the rarity of copies that survive into the twenty-first century as valuable antiques.

GAI: That is weird, when you think about it.

RES: While not the cheapest of pamphlets or chapbooks, *The Pilgrim's Progress* was not originally aimed at the cultural elite. Bunyan's circle of nonconformists would certainly have included a wide social range, but the majority would be of the poorer kind. Bunyan had already established his reputation as a writer of religious polemic by the time *The Pilgrim's Progress* was published. But with this book, he became a best-seller. Hence the multiple editions, all printed by Nathaniel Ponder, from 1678 to 1688, the time of Bunyan's death. *The Pilgrim's Progress* is sometimes mentioned in accounts of the birth of the English novel for its realist dialogue and narrative characterization. But its market placement in 1678 is not among a welter of literary fiction. Rather it is published by a notorious printer of non-conformist religious books and tracts. This same market placement continues through to today.

GH: We noticed how many of the books were published by religious presses.

RES: But the book's fortunes change. From a period of disrepute in literary circles, where even religious allies like the poet and hymnist William Cowper refused to actually name Bunyan in his commendation, *The Pilgrim's Progress* is said to start to gain literary approval with the English Poet Laureate, Robert Southey's *Life of Bunyan* introducing an 1830 edition.

GAI: And it seems that once that respectability you mentioned kicks in the publications get more prestigious in size and décor.

MNA: And, actually, more varied. An increased drive for schooling in the industrial political economy also generated a need for a corpus of canonical texts for studying literature.

GAI: And Bunyan fits the bill of the good honest Englishman of the people. He gets called upon as a pioneer of popular expression in the movement toward the modern novel. So, we've seen book copies in this pile that are explicitly set out as texts for educational purposes. They have comprehension questions for each chapter at the back, with notes on vocabulary and grammar for students.

RES: So, the twentieth century sees a real diversity in publication strategies oriented to the general market. *The Pilgrim's Progress* is sold as a literary classic for the consumer wanting to be well-read, as well as a spiritual classic for the religious market in an increasingly secularized society. And publishers also, I suspect, appreciate a steady-seller that requires neither royalties nor much marketing investment for small presses. And then the push to greater access to university education further bolsters the textbook status of the book with Early Modern studies, literature, and history. Eventually, reaching the pinnacle of intellectual refinement or appropriation, depending on how you look at it, you get the foundation of a scholarly guild in the 1980s, the International John Bunyan Society, which publishes a learned journal, a newsletter and hosts conferences.

GAI: Can I just go back to one detail of Mnason's point about the school books?

RES: Sure.

MNA: What is it?

GAI: You mentioned chapters, but Bunyan didn't write in chapters at all, in neither Part I nor Part II.

MNA: Good point. But it didn't take too long for editors to take the text in hand to try to discipline it.

RES: Why do you think that happened?

MNA: My suspicion is that it has to do with the use of the book for religious instruction. You get a whole host of clergy devoting mid-week church meetings to teaching *The Pilgrim's Progress*. A number of those series of lectures or sermons were published. One of the earliest dividers of the text was an English engraver turned minister called George Burder. He published an edition of *The Pilgrim's Progress* divided into chapters. Later these divisions get renamed as stages, as in stages of the journey, presumably.

GH: It could also have to do with reading habits. Notice the technological concern of a certain Tom Fenton's recent Amazon.com review of an independently published "Unabridged" edition. He writes, "Totally unreadable; NOT AT ALL comparable to the Kindle 'UNABRIDGED' VERSION. There are NO CHAPTER DESIGNATIONS or location markers in the print copy. Therefore, EITHER THE KINDLE OR THIS PRINT COPY, OR BOTH are fraudulent in their claim to be 'unabridged.' I am thoroughly disappointed. I wanted to alternate reading the Kindle & the print copy but it is impossible to find my place in this print copy."

GAI: Oh, so that explains how the text is divided up online or in some audiobooks, even though the divisions don't go back to Bunyan. But it's worth noting that when it comes to making those divisions there is also no settled pattern as to how many chapters to break the text up into.

MNA: We also see the preaching commentary seeping into the books alongside the text. Burder uses the chapter breaks to offer his own commentary and then start the next with his summary of the action to come.

GH: John Newton was an early editorial annotator. One of the most extensively reprinted is William Mason. It's up there with Thomas Scott. Later in the nineteenth century, campaigning anti-slavery American clergyman, George Cheever, lectures extensively on the book, and furnishes notes to printed editions.

MNA: The most magisterial nineteenth-century commentator is George Offor. He produced one of the earliest text-critical scholarly editions, indicating how the text had experienced change through its editions. This was for the Baptist historical Hanserd Knollys Society.

GAI: Did you know that Offor had a massive collection of Bunyan material in his personal library and that it was nearly all tragically destroyed by an auction house fire in 1865?

MNA: That's such a shame, in one way. But in another, it doesn't seem to have inhibited on-going enthusiasm for the book.

GH: But editors do have an impact on the reading of the book, surely?

RES: How so, do you think?

GH: Well, it seems that one editorial strategy is to connect the text of *The Pilgrim's Progress* to a biography or even the autobiography of the author.

MNA: By autobiography, you mean Bunyan's 1666 *Grace Abounding to the Chief of Sinners*.

GH: Yes. And in either instance, it seems that the reader, while doing this pre-reading, or even just skipping a lot of pages to get to the story, will be led to think that the particular life of the author must have a bearing on the text. Something not so obviously found if you were to read Dickens, Austen, or Stephen King.

GAI: Go on.

GH: I suppose the reader is being told that the book's autobiographical echoes from a venerated Christian's life should shape their reading approach and disposition in response to the text.

RES: Could we say this is a highly orchestrated version of the frontispiece illustration by Robert White of Bunyan as a dreaming author above a lion in the mouth of a cave, half-sealed by a portcullis? That image, after all, speaks of the author's notorious political imprisonment as a dissenter that does the same tie in to the narrative of the burdened Christian depicted leaving the City of Destruction in the upper background.

GH: And readers might also be led to think of the author as a dreamer, akin to the biblical prophet Daniel in authority, with the visual nod to the lions' den.

RES: Good point.

MNA: Still the direction of an editor's flowery praise of Bunyan is a bit more heavy-handed in fifty pages of text rather than in one image.

RES: Good point, and well made.

GAI: I guess what we're getting at here is that editors and publishers frame how the text is accessed and to whom it is marketed and for what purposes.

GH: And how it will be interpreted once read. Remember those marginal Bible references. Well, in keeping with educational standards, these often become footnotes. But footnotes do a different job for the reader. No longer alongside the text but rather below it, they will now play a subordinate role. They do the footnote job of indicating supportive authority without eliciting a discontinuous reading.

GAI: Fancy wording, GH. You're starting to sound like Researcher! But there's also the opposite problem. Some of the nineteenth-century editors are so wordy in their annotations that their notes often compete for space on the page.

MNA: And there's definitely a paternalistic confidence in the way they address the "dear reader" as assumed Christians. They suppose their readers all want to avoid the errors that strew the journey. These editors often seem to vie to even outdo Bunyan's orthodoxy in attacking the looseness of false Christians or whole denominations or expressions of Christianity.

GH: Yet, that same type of expression does have an undisguised sincerity in seeking to communicate a spiritual good to readers. These annotations don't think the gospel of justification in Christ is a neutral commodity to observe, still less to neglect or explain away as a religious bygone of former times.

RES: So, the positioning of Bunyan's text in relation to his own relocated notes and references, and to the front-matter and end-matter that surrounds the text, well, matters, right?

GAI: Yes, and this is made all the more obvious when publishers start having editor's annotations included in their book copies, as we've already mentioned. At first these were preachers and theologians. Their notes might be reproduced from their stand-alone lectures or sermons on the book. It has been noted that they tend to offer a polemical interpretation, often in support of Bunyan's theological emphases, to a later readership that does not overwhelmingly share the same emphases. So, notes by John Newton, William Mason, George Burder, or Scott Thomas all give vigorous defenses of the importance of salvation as justification by grace through faith, often underlining and simply repeating, rewording or expanding Bunyan's own teaching point in their notes. But they also do this with the confidence that the reader shares their religious disposition. They address the reader directly with exclamations, encouragements and sober warnings. George Offor's mid-nineteenth-century annotated *Pilgrim's Progress* is still in print. In it, he collates his top picks of the commentaries of his forebears in the evangelical faith, so it's a good one stop shop to get a feel for these annotation traditions.

GH: We should also recognize that book copies are not just produced with religious enthusiasm in view.

MNA: Editorial notes also appear as the book gets increasing academic respect for use in the classroom and in scholarship. As it happens, George Offor was one of the first to explicitly lay out the apparatus of a scholarly text with his 1843 edition. He noted which bits of text and marginal notes were from which edition. By the end of the nineteenth century editions also come with notes explaining vocabulary and grammatical forms that would be unfamiliar to the reader. Literary editions today have extensive glossaries for word meaning, as well as notes that explain possible influences for Bunyan's imagination. Like the fact that we know that Bunyan knew the desperate account of the apostatizing Italian Protestant, Francis Spira, and his anxiety driven death. The misery of the man in the iron cage can be connected to this same eventual fate. We know this because Bunyan mentions Spira in his earlier autobiography.

GAI: And then there are notes that locate Bunyan's language in the wider flow of published English, looking back to Shakespeare or to collections of contemporary emblems where text and picture are joined to showcase the religion of the day.

GH: And schoolbook editions locate Bunyan within the canon of literature a student should be expected to know. So, an early twentieth-century editor notes that the three Shining Ones at the cross are reminiscent of Dante's angelic hosts through purgatory. It is the literary reader who will benefit from such a connection, even though the observation is far from the intent of Bunyan's religious encouragement of dissenting Christians as he wrote, or from their likely literary interests.

MNA: But if notes add visibly to the text, what about more subtle and invisible editorializing in changing the text for a more modernized read?

GH: There will be some variety of opinion on this according to someone's view of the purpose of reading the book in the first place.

GAI: Go on.

GH: Buying the book as a spiritual classic for religious self-edification or gifting it to another would suggest that there is a message in the text that is patient of translation, without loss to the message. So Modernized English versions function as translations, even though the language is technically the same.

GAI: I did find out about translations into foreign languages, too.

GH: Let's get to them once we've reported on the Modernized English versions.

MNA: How about we recognize why these might be called for. I think it's clear that seventeenth-century English is not everyone's cup of tea.

RES: Yes, it can be a struggle for my students, although I do tell them that a good audiobook will make the meaning come out more clearly. Something about the read aloud experience can convey meaning in intonation, deft handling of long sentences, and simple pacing, where the text would otherwise challenge habitual forms of encounter with text.

GAI: Are you saying that texting, social media, and online scrolling are poor trainers of reading skills?

RES: I did not say that.

GH: Anyway . . . Mnason, you were going to lead our report here.

MNA: Right. So, the goal of a modernized English version is going to be to preserve the story while making it more accessible to readers. We're not talking about abridgement here, by the way. That's a different way of making the text accessible.

GAI: Can you give us some examples?

MNA: Sure. When Faithful is being accused at trial in Vanity, one of his accusers if called Pickthank. He follows Suspicion and Envy. Their names don't present a problem but his does. Scholarly editions have to give an explanatory note, to the effect that to be a pickthank is to be someone who ingratiates themselves to their superiors, sucking up to them to gain their favor and gratitude—picking thanks from them, as it were. While quite a few modernized versions keep his original name, variations offered are variously: Mr. Talebearer, Deception, Gainglory or Flattery. This change of name makes sense, I think, because the name is not so distinctively integral to the character encounter that any of these others cannot suffice. A similar, earlier expression in need of updating comes when Christian refers to the "children of my bowels," meaning of his deepest, heartfelt affection. Most modernizations simply eliminate the qualification of the children by co-opting them into the earlier "dear" that Christian attaches to his wife. But one replaces "of my bowels" with "the fruit of my own body" which ends up misreading bowels as a physical claim rather than one of emotion and affection.

GH: Although you might admit that physical bonds imply emotional ones, no?

MNA: Ok, fair enough. In the same passage Bunyan writes of the City of Destruction's "fearful overthrow," and in doing so he is silently quoting from Genesis 19 where the fate of Sodom and Gomorrah narratively frame this opening section. Modernizations lose that word "overthrow," but before we get too critical, this has already happened with some modern Bible translations of Genesis 19, which use the words "destroy" or "demolish" instead. We're talking about details that matter to those who think the details matter to experience the pleasure of Bunyan's composition. This is in contrast to those who think this level of detail can change without impact on the experience of pleasure at the engagement of Bunyan's story.

RES: Right. You are not going to be reading a modernized version comparatively with a seventeenth-century text, because the whole point is that you didn't want that kind of textual struggle.

MNA: How about a modernization that obscures a deeper theological point of interpretation? Let's consider that Christian finds his key of Promise to escape Doubting Castle in Bunyan's words, in his "bosom." But that word "bosom" has changed and largely lost its meaning. While it can mean the human breast, it has mostly become uniformly feminized. That means modern readers find it hard to imagine Christian even having a bosom. However, keeping something in one's bosom denotes both physical space and spiritual importance. It's not hard to see that keeping something by one's bosom is keeping it close to one's heart. The lingering phrase of "bosom buddies" gets at the emotional tone somewhat. Likely, the bosom location is a fold, pouch or pocket in upper body clothing. You might think about the bosom as the upper body equivalent of the lap. A lap is related to the body without being a body part. The lap is present when sitting and not when standing. The bosom is present when the arm embraces the chest, or a fold of clothing envelopes the upper body, without being the breast literally. Nevertheless, the use of "bosom" here reminds readers that this is where Christian has stored or failed to store his roll from which he takes encouraging reads as he travels. So, the key and the roll, and the book before them, stand for the Bible to which then "bosom" stands in both senses as a physical location in the folds of clothing around one's chest as well as the spiritual sense of close to one's heart (already used metaphorically). Modernized English versions have to adapt. One version replaces "bosom" with chest pocket at consistent points of the journey, which gets at the correct anatomical location, but struggles with the spiritual sense. Another puts the scroll "hidden in his coat, close to his heart" but when the key is found in Doubting Castle it is merely located in his "pocket." Another locates the key in a "pocket close to his heart," but had previously used the words "chest pocket" which loses the connection some. Interestingly some, perhaps in thinking of bosom buddies, keep the old word trusting modern readers to keep up with the imagery.

RES: I'm starting to think that there's a murky overlap at the boundary between modernization as translation and as adaptation. But I do want to point out that modernization is not the same thing as abridgement. Modernization is an adaptation that might be judged to lose meaning but does not intend to do so. Abridgement is the deliberate cutting of the text to enable anything from cheaper printing and therefore lower cost to the customer, to the removal of overly complex material that would puzzle readers, and then the removal of material of which the abridger disapproves so that, effectively, it is as if it were never in the book in the first place. The most famous abridger of *The Pilgrim's Progress* is the eighteenth-century founder of Methodism, John Wesley. He included a version of *Pilgrim's Progress* in his 1750 *Christian Library* of improving works for Christian readers. Wesley keeps all major narrative events but often chops dialogue to abbreviate the text. His theological persuasion, against a predestinarian gospel of sovereign grace, is shown in the excising and editing of Christian's conversation with the man in the iron cage. No longer does the man tell Christian that "God hath denied me repentance; his word gives me no encouragement to believe, yea he himself has shut me up in this iron cage." Rather the man's explanation for his not repenting is about his own actions: "For I have quenched the Spirit." This is followed by the exclamation, "O Eternity, Eternity! who can tell the length of Eternity?" whereas Bunyan had written with a much clearer judgment, "O eternity; eternity! How shall I grapple with the misery that I must meet with in eternity?"

GAI: So, Wesley's abridgment is also a silent re-write at some points?

RES: Yes.

MNA: Ok, but while we're on the silent re-write theme, I also noticed that a few modernizations had removed Bunyan's reference to the Flatterer's black flesh. I reckon that's a good thing, seeing as how his skin color is unnecessary to flesh out the Proverbs 29:5 that Bunyan is visually illustrating. These rewrites also cut out the racist imagination that sees the Devil as black, and then slips into seeing black skin as devilish.

GAI: It does get to the point of what it is modernizers or even abridgers think they are being faithful to in their tinkering. If it's faithfulness to Bunyan's words in modern guise you might, as has been done, change "black of flesh" to "with black skin." However, if you think faithfulness is to the gospel and that the Bible has no place for racist portrayals, you might remove the reference to skin color altogether, on the basis that the danger of succumbing to false teaching and flattery is not a racial issue. Faithfulness to biblical truth calls out Bunyan's unfaithful vision in this instance.

MNA: Of course, that does leave the publisher or editor open to a charge of white-washing over past failures of a Christian tradition that ought to be part of a warts-and-all reception of a spiritual classic.

RES: In the same way, Wesley might feel justified by the same faithfulness to the gospel as he reduces the visibility of Bunyan's more Calvinist theological moves. But again, with Mnason, that does leave him liable for altering a theological text to portray it as closer to his interpretation of the Bible than it actually was.

GH: So much of what we're seeing in these book copies is that the intended purpose and readership for a book affects the decisions made about the presentation of the text and its original marginal apparatus.

GAI: And as I mentioned earlier, that readership goes far beyond the modern reader of English. The book was very quickly being translated in other languages. Bunyan reports in his preface to Part II that Part I was already received in France and Holland. It was soon translated into Welsh. Its use by English missionaries over the next centuries brought it into over two hundred languages across the entire world.

RES: We'll explore its use in missions in another trip.

GH: Gaius may be saying that our climb could have been a lot higher had it included editions in other languages!

MNA: It was high enough for me.

GAI: But we did have a few translations here, did you not notice? Didn't you see the range of French translations or that in the last fifteen years there have been at least five new and different Brazilian Portuguese translations.

RES: The fact is, though, good Gaius, that the English-speaking readers of this research project may not care about translations. Maybe we'll find time for them later on, but for now, I've got more than enough material for unpacking the book dimension of the Pilgrimverse.

 I saw in my dream that Gaius, visibly sulking, slunk away, muttering to himself. Great-Heart at last relaxed and holstered his sword, while Mnason sat down for a rest and immediately looked panicked when he realized that Gaius had taken the snacks with him. As I awoke, he started pestering Great-Heart to lead him anywhere where they might find food.

NAR: So, Researcher, what do you make of these findings?

RES: I'm pretty impressed with the scope and the details these guys dug up. It does seem to indicate that it's hard to say there is only one Pilgrim's Progress.

NAR: So well before the Pilgrimverse welcomed movies or board game adaptations, it was almost from the outset diverse.

RES: So it appears.

NAR: That helps me weave in Proverbs 11:1 from the top of the chapter. As you gather information from more and more of the Pilgrimverse you will, I think, inevitably come to form judgements over the honesty of editors' and adapters' scales, metaphorically used to measure *The Pilgrim's Progress*.

RES: And while I can't presume to throw God's judgment of favor or detestation around, there may be ways to map how different groups of Christians and even non-Christians receive and present the book as text as a reflection on their own perspective on God's judgment in the former case, or from the perspective of literary or historical or sociopolitical judgment in the latter.

NAR: And it might be worth pointing out that neither of those receptions have to be strictly mutually exclusive.

RES: Hmm, wise words. There's some complexity here. More navigation of the Pilgrimverse will help us, for sure. Now where is Gaius with those snacks?

Pilgrimverse Resources

Bunyan, John. *The Pilgrim's Progress [. . .]* Abridged by John Wesley. Newcastle Upon Tyne: John Gooding, 1743.

Bunyan, John. *The Pilgrim's Progress From This World to That Which Is to Come Delivered in the Similitude of a Dream, A New Edition, Divided into Chapters, to Which Are Added Explanatory and Practical Notes [. . .]* by G. Burder. Coventry: M. Luckman, 1786.

Bunyan, John. *The Works of John Bunyan*. 3 vols. Edited by George Offor. Grand Rapids: Baker, 1977.

3

Comics

Dear friend, you are faithful in what you are doing for the brothers and sisters, even though they are strangers to you.

3 JOHN 5

In my dream I saw Faithful and Hopeful approach a pile of graphic novels. The pile was uneven as these varied in size and bulk and production finish. Fortunately, this wasn't too crowded a field of adaptation so the climb to the top of pile was more of a hop, skip, and a jump than the mountaineering effort for the editions and translations Great-heart and friends had navigated. The Researcher had gathered eleven different versions, 7 in English, and 4 in Korean. But there was no sign of him in the office. Faithful pulled out the map they had been given earlier.

FAI: Look, Hopeful, I can see on the map that the first trip, which we missed, was up over that mountain of books over there.

HOP: Right. So where should we head, then? I thought Researcher would be here to greet us. The others said he helped them out with guidelines before they set out.

FAI: Well, he's not here now. Perhaps he's off teaching a class. But it doesn't matter, we have the map.

HOP: And it's this pile next, is it?

Comics

On top of the pile was a brightly colored Marvel comic from 1992, produced in collaboration with Christian publishers Thomas Nelson. The cover image was of Christian, armor-clad and built with the arms of a body-builder, wielding his sword upwards at a deep green, yellow clawed and red-eyed Dragon, equally muscular but four times his size. Faithful started to hang back. He looked unsure that this adventure would be a good idea. (Little did he know the discomfort it would bring to Hopeful.)

FAI: I'm not sure that a comic is the best format for this mature work of Protestant spiritual imagination. *The Pilgrim's Progress* is a work deeply embedded in the word. In fact, Bunyan warns readers not to get caught up in the imagery so as to lose the true gospel message.

HOP: Are you not just saying that 'cos you're afraid of that beast? To be honest, I'm kind of with you on that . . .

FAI (ignoring Hopeful): This is what Bunyan says:
Take heed also, that thou be not extreme,
In playing with the outside of my dream:
Nor let my figure or similitude
Put thee into a laughter or a feud;
Leave this for Boys *and* Fools; *but as for thee,*
Do thou the substance of my matter see.

And the substance is the gospel truth about salvation in Jesus Christ and a life lived by faith.

HOP: So are you concerned that an image based rendition of *The Pilgrim's Progress* must of necessity draw focus away from the underlying message? That it will focus too much on the adornment that Bunyan wove in metaphors that now gets set in color?

FAI: Exactly. So, I'm really not sure about going forward. Plus, it does look a little scary.

HOP: I get that you, of all people, might carry around an anxiety about an imminent death, but we are agents of the Researcher and we know Gaius and Mnason came back just fine from their trip.

FAI: Don't forget they had Great-Heart and his whopping great sword with them, too, though.

HOP: I'm not forgetting. Ah, here comes Researcher! Help me out here, will you?

RES: What with?

HOP: Faithful's worried this graphic novel domain of the Pilgrimverse could be dangerous. I said we'd be fine.

FAI (muttering): Look at you, Mr Glass half-full!

RES: Actually, Hopeful's right. You should be perfectly safe. At the end of the day, these are just illustrations you'll be exploring. 2-D doesn't bite.

FAI: But don't you think that nothing is more likely to get us distracted from the right message of Pilgrim's Progress than the lurid color of a bunch of comics?

HOP: Well, hold on a minute. Technically, probably only two on this pile should even qualify as comics. The others would nowadays be gathered under the genre of graphic novel.

FAI: Isn't that just a comic for grown-ups who should know better?

HOP: Maybe we ought to check these out before dismissing them too readily. In any case, maybe it will do us good to read image and not just text for a while.

FAI: And how are we distinguishing this pile of visual works from other illustrated editions of *The Pilgrim's Progress*?

RES: I suspect there's a little bit of ambiguity around the edges, but let's suppose a graphic novel sets any text (as speech, thought, or narration) within the overall and dominant frame of visual depiction of action, event, setting, characterization, and state of mind, that moves sequentially from frame to frame.

FAI: And conversely, how would we describe illustrations?

RES: Well, I suspect that it's easiest to say that you know an illustration when you see one!

HOP: Fair enough.

FAI: I'm just wanting to check out the definitions.

RES: Ok, so, early on in the Pilgrimverse images are produced on separate pages inserted amid the printed pages of text. These are known as plates. The whole page is given over to inked images made from woodcuts or engravings. Later on, as production techniques change, these plates get more elaborate and are sometimes kept pristine in a fancy version of the book by a tissue paper insert. But eventually printing technology develops so that drawings can be embedded within the text of any page as little vignettes. But you guys can just stick to using the term illustration, when it comes to it later, I think.

FAI: OK. I reckon we should be able to tell the difference—more image than text is a graphic novel or comic—more text than image is an illustrated book.

RES: That will certainly do.

HOP: All right. I think we can set off. But while we're gone, could you put your thinking cap on, Mr. Researcher? Because, aren't Puritan Protestants like Bunyan supposed to dislike images? Even to the extent of destroying them, you know, being iconoclasts?

FAI (aside to Hopeful): Researcher may be a poor judge on that. After all he's happily employing our visual selves for his own gain—could be a case of conflict of interest and unacknowledged bias, but we can see what he says, I suppose.

As they examined the Marvel comics cover more closely, they discerned the hinges of the portal along the spine of the title "P"s. Together they prized the title upwards as if a trapdoor and both jumped through the resulting hole opening onto a swirl of colors that was the portal into the Pilgrimverse's graphic novel dimension. Their previous experience of jumping out of books gave both Faithful and Hopeful confidence, this time around, that their book hopping could go smoothly. It was still a shock when they found themselves landing in the Valley of Humiliation with, effectively, ringside seats to Christian's battle with Apollyon

The first thing they noticed after jumping in from Marvel's cover, was that the Christian inside the comic wasn't quite as colossally heroic in stature as the cover promised. The cover image had been, for want to a better phrase, beefed up. The inside Christian was still wearing his shirt sleeves when fighting Apollyon and not parading colossal biceps as the cover promised.

FAI: Typical cover image touch up!

HOP: Let's not stay in this hot spot for longer than necessary. How are we assessing what we see?

FAI: Let's just hang back here so we don't get caught in the fight that's about to kick off.

HOP: We know Christian isn't going to turn back to see us. He's got no armor on his back!

FAI: Right, so just keep out of Apollyon's eye line, then. These rocks should shield us. Ok, so let's think what we want to look out for. Apollyon's appearance should fit Bunyan's description, right?

HOP: Or we could see how it might fit conventions of monstrosity that communicate evil in other ways?

FAI: Sure. Then we need to see if the encounter itself is driven by dialogue charged with Apollyon's spiritual mockery and outrage at Christian's spurning his claims of lordship.

FAI: Right, so let's bear in mind that Bunyan makes the majority of this encounter of Christian and Apollyon a war of words rather than actual fight.

HOP: Well, that's true in terms of words on the page, but he does show that much more time passed during the fight then in the conversation.

FAI: So we could see how the extent of the battle is portrayed. Bunyan noted that it "lasted for above half a day, even till Christian was almost quite spent."

HOP: So one thing to consider is the ways that Bunyan's narration of time passing is conveyed visually?

FAI: That's right. Without a narrator, time in graphic novels passes in the movement within and between the panels. The gutter between panels can be used to convey faster or slower time passage according to its visual framing.

HOP: Huh. You've given this some thought, I see!

FAI: Thanks. Lastly, we should pay attention to how the battle ends and what Apollyon's defeat looks like.

The conversation between Christian and Apollyon that they had been keeping an eye on as they planned their criteria of evaluation seemed to be getting very heated.

HOP: Ok, ok. I think Christian's pushing things past the talking stage right now. . . . How'd you fancy some book hopping to get the lie of the graphic novel Pilgrimverse zone? We could collect some overall impressions of how each adaptation allocates resources to this encounter before we end up getting ourselves too close to the action?

FAI: Yeah, I'm happy leaving them to it in here once we've grabbed a few stats. So, for a starter, Marvel is distinctive in telling the story of both Part I and Part II in the same volume, whereas all the others only cover Part I.

HOP: Even then, Part II only gets seventeen of the ninety-two total pages.

FAI: Well observed. Now as to the battle with Apollyon, we know Bunyan gave less than 3 percent of his narrative over to this episode. We surely are going to expect that this percentage will increase in the visual field of comics that, particularly in a superhero stable such as Marvel, are driven by action and combat.

HOP: Yes, Marvel in fact gives seven pages of their seventy-five-page depiction of Part I to the battle, up near the 10 percent mark. And they definitely follow Bunyan's dragon language in their depiction of Apollyon.

FAI: How does Bunyan put it again?

HOP: "[T]he monster was hideous to behold. He was clothed with scales, like a fish (and they are his pride). He had wings like a dragon, feet like a bear, and out of his belly came fire and smoke, and his mouth was as the mouth of a lion."

FAI: So, Marvel is faithful to the detail about the belly in that they have a fang-lined mouth opening up in the beast's stomach to then capture Christian with a serpent-like tongue.

HOP: I can see that. But they don't have the monstrosity of a creature of mixed parts, there are no scales, bear paws or lion's mouth.

FAI: But evil is conveyed in color. The monster is green! A tell-tale stereotype of monstrosity, think the Wicked Witch of the West.

HOP: Or the Hulk, or the Grinch, or Shrek . . .

FAI: All right, back off, I don't think those are so helpful for my point. Marvel also give their dragon red eyes. Those aren't Bunyan details but they fit typical expectations of evil in the form of a beast.

HOP: So, the episode is given a higher narrative profile. The diabolical evil is well communicated. Enough said for now?

FAI: Yeah, let's get out of here.

    I saw in my dream that the two then moved through the pile of graphic novels, scanning for similar comparative details. They emerged back through the Marvel title portal in a slightly indecent hurry to compare notes just as the Researcher was approaching his desk.

RES: How's it going?

FAI: We could have stayed longer, the artwork really draws you in, you know? But we navigated quickly and have gathered some comparisons that might be interesting.

HOP: And we were scared of the battle scenes.

FAI: Oh, and that, hence the speed, yes.

HOP: This bit of the Pilgrimverse has quite a lot of jurisdictional overlap with illustrations, as you mentioned earlier.

FAI: We decided that the books that present *The Pilgrim's Progress* with serial visual panels with running text narrative flowing under each panel did not qualify as graphic novels. It's a little ambiguous, but the format and design leans more toward heavy illustration of an abridged text than true comics style. So, that ruled out mid-twentieth-century books like *The Pilgrim's Progress in Pictures* and *Pictorial Pilgrim's Progress*.

RES: Fair enough. So what's the scoop?

FAI: Did you check out the whole thing about images being acceptable or not?

RES: I did. Tell me what you've found out, and then I'll let you know what I've found in answer to your question about images and iconoclasm.

HOP: All right.
   Both characters explained to Researcher the criteria of their comparison.

FAI: Marvel makes the battle a larger part of the narrative as an action comic and shows some faithfulness in representing Apollyon as monstrously evil.

HOP: Al Bohl's 1994 Barbour Christian Comics version is much slenderer at only thirty-seven pages, of which three are given to the battle. So that's a similar profile to Marvel, at eight and a bit percent of total pages.

FAI: His Apollyon is more textually faithful with a lion's head, bear's feet and covered in scales.

HOP: Green scales, by the way. And, of course, massive dragon wings.

FAI: The fire is being breathed from his mouth rather than his stomach, though. Steve Vossos in his three-volume, self-published graphic novel also gets the animal parts to fit.

FAI: Well, he kind of has to, as he hand writes every word of Bunyan's text into his panels.

HOP: That is an amazing feature of his graphic novel. This encounter, by the way, still takes up four out of the full ninety pages of his combined volumes. That's not much more than 4 percent so much closer to the weight of exposure that Bunyan's text grants. Even so, he doesn't have any belly emissions in his drawings.

RES: It is a weird bit of imagery, you have to admit.

FAI: Fair comment. And there's also no green. Or color at all, for that matter. Vossos uses black ink alone for text and image, giving his work a proximity to the original woodcuts that adorned early editions of *The Pilgrim's Progress*.

FAI: For the record, we should acknowledge that although Bunyan doesn't give his Apollyon source references, he's clearly drawing on Leviathan in Job 40 and 41, as well as on Revelation 12 and 13 for the dragon and mixed-matched beast components.

RES: And in fairness to the dragon illustrators, the Bible's Job has the fire coming from Leviathan's mouth too, not, like Bunyan, from his belly.

HOP: So you're saying that illustrators who don't follow Bunyan's belly thing are being more biblically faithful?

FAI: Perhaps so, ironically . . .

RES: Who else have you got?

HOP: Stephen Moore has an Apollyon who morphs from a crowned human king-like figure, who torments Christian as Bunyan represents in his dialogue, to a greenish muscular dragon monster. Two prominent horns must be meant to represent the figure visually as Satanic, following convention. His encounter takes up just under 6 percent of his page count.

FAI: Lee Tung and Johnny Wong's two-volume manga was produced in China, but the English version is put out by Kingstone Comics in the US. They give thirteen pages out of their whopping 302 to the incident, just over 4 percent. Like Vossos, that's getting down to the proportion Bunyan originally allocated. Their Apollyon is also a super muscular two-horned dragon monster with giant wings. It's a human inflected dragon, rather than the animal combo of Bunyan's description, but it too morphs.

HOP: Right, the encounter with Apollyon includes a temptation sequence where "Suddenly Apollyon changes to a very beautiful woman." That's a little creepy, but maybe we should save comment on that to another time.

FAI: Sure, let's mention the monumental, 2019, three-volume graphic novel by Chol-Kyu Choi. It packs a colossal 662 pages of visual adaptation. So, when the Apollyon encounter takes up eighteen pages, the longest treatment in these comics, it still represents less than 3 percent of full treatment, exactly consistent with the balance of Bunyan's text. His Apollyon does have, no surprise, green scales when examined close up, and emits fire from his belly. But bear's feet and lion's mouth are not portrayed. But this is a clearly satanic-dragon, a two horned winged monster who touts a trident as a weapon, like the stereotypical devil's pitchfork of Halloween costumes.

HOP: Not a detail that Bunyan includes, as fiery darts are the weapons of his beast, in keeping with Ephesians 6:16.

RES: Thanks guys. I've got a sense that this genre of adaptation has different modes of demonstrating creativity and fidelity to the source text. You asked me about the theology of using images at all. Maybe I can fill you in a bit before I ask you to give me your sense of how the theological aspects of this battle with Apollyon are represented.

FAI: Wait, there's one more adaptation we've skipped over.

RES: Which is that?

HOP: It's by Ralph Sanders, and it offers a pretty different visual interpretation than these others. Rather than representation of Bunyan's narrative, it doubles down on metaphor by reframing the adventure as one by a motorcyclist riding through a dark, dystopian modernity meeting the anthropomorphized animals who inhabit it.

RES: I know it, and yes, it is pretty different. Let's come back to Sanders toward the end of our conversation. I've had some thoughts on it. For now, let's take a big picture view of the relation of Bunyan's flavor of theology and visual art.

FAI and HOP: OK, Go for it.

RES: So, you're right to associate Protestants, and Puritans as a stricter sort of Protestant, with iconoclasm, or the distrust of and even destruction of images, particularly in places of worship. This has to do with the cultural emergence of a Word-based, Bible and preaching centered Protestant Christianity from a Reformation that rejected intermediaries in salvation such that intermediary visual aids to worship and devotion fell under suspicion of false religion. And, by the way, Bunyan himself lives in a day where Catholics are religious and political enemies of England in its European setting. This is manifest popularly in suspicion that Catholics had plotted to burn down London in its great fire of 1666, and in on-going concern that Charles the II's marriage to Catholic Catherine of Braganza of Portugal would lead to a national coup taking the nation back to Catholicism, as nearly happened with the accession of James II just after Bunyan's death. All of which is to say that images could be problematic, in fact and by association, to the Protestant mind.

FAI: That's why Pope turns up briefly in Part I as a not very, but still attempting to be, scary Giant?

RES: Yes, and why Vanity Fair's chief sales are in the "wares of Rome" from which only "our English nation" has successfully thrown off the allure.

HOP: Oh, yes, I remember, those were the parts Mnason and Gaius told me were missed out of the French translation in the 1780s, right?

RES: Exactly. Anyhow, back to images. We know that Luther had an outsize impact on Bunyan theologically, given the centrality of justification through faith in the Pilgrimverse. It may be that Luther's attitude to creative imagery rubbed off somewhat too. Luther held images to be of secondary importance, and beneficial to the extent that, with, for example, Albrecht Durer's woodcuts, they could illustrate the proclaimed word of gospel preaching. Luther indeed opposes the more radical iconoclasts in his own circles at Wittenberg. Nevertheless, within a generation, Calvin, showing great familiarity with Patristic sources and early church debates on the question, ensures that images would have no part in worship. The Protestants who shape English and eventually American Christianity are confirmed as a people who are hearers of the word not gazers at images, or more pointedly, idols. For Bunyan's English context, Reformers are behind the sustained destruction of monasteries and stripping of the altars and rood screens from parish churches. This state-orchestrated and individually-motivated purging of visual space for the word proclaimed and written, along with, at times, virulent anti-Catholic nationalism, gives Bunyan his cultural inheritance.

FAI: So a graphic novel dimension of the Pilgrimverse is also suspicious, do you think?

RES: Well, where you have an intensely word-based religious piety that is suspicious of images you should expect a potential clash with an artform that gives images dominance over words in the shape of comics and graphic novels.

HOP: So, we're interested in finding out if adaptations of a classic from this supposedly iconoclastic or even iconophobic religious tradition, are valid?

RES: My sense is that once Bunyan chooses to depict his vision of the Christian life in allegory, through the conceit of a narrated dream, he fuels an imaginary that is always open to visual representation.

FAI: An imaginary?

RES: Sorry, that's a fancy short-hand word for a way of being in the world that supplies all the possibilities for imagination. So, the fact that Bunyan uses verbal illustrations and narrative enactments of biblical texts could or even should open up his readers to the possibility that those verbal illustrations take visual form. Like a natural imaginative development.

HOP: I'm with you so far, go on.

RES: As you know, Bunyan's opening verse apology for *The Pilgrim's Progress* recognizes that his falling into allegory poses a problem to some godly readers. For some of his contemporaries, truth was truth and ought not be embellished with fiction, or in other words, falsehood. Bunyan at length shows how Scripture itself, the prophets and even Jesus use metaphors or in his terms, similitudes, to better draw. His conclusion at the close of Part I is therefore significant. Having desired that his book should make a travailer or traveler out of the reader, he warns lest the journey into imaginative realms blind the pilgrim reader to the underlying spiritual message of his allegory.

FAI: We were talking about that just a little earlier.

RES: Good. On the one hand, we can note that setting out his allegories in the parts of characters is a strong echo of the craft of playwrights who draw on the common morality play tradition with its stock visual characters.

HOP: "Everyman" and other characters in a play are like cartoon characters before cartoons, as it were.

RES: Sure, but on the other hand, Bunyan does not make an argument for concrete visual images.

FAI: So where does that leave us?

RES: I think I can, like others before me, make a stab at a theology with which Bunyan could sympathize.

HOP: Hit us up!

RES: Ok. It goes like this: The incarnation of the eternally begotten Son of God, God made flesh, is the most straight forward theological entry way into a defense of images.

FAI: I love it when the answer is Jesus!

RES: Good! The one who is the image of the invisible God is come near and at hand, visibly. The present and eternal significance of the eternal incarnation of the now ascended and glorified Christ signifies the abiding presence of created humanity in the full presence of God. The pointers of the incarnation, not least in the Gospel of John's prologue, back to creation and forward to the redemption of all things, sustains a confidence in the visual material goodness of creation, whose substance and form will be redeemed by glorification and purification but not effaced by apocalyptic judgment.

HOP: Slow down a bit, let me just take that in.

RES: (barely pausing) The imagination of the Heavenly Jerusalem in Revelation that funds Bunyan's destination of the Celestial City itself borrows heavily as it adapts previous prophetic oracles. Ultimately, it is an incarnation-warranted security of human imaging that grounds the possibility and freedom of graphic depiction of humans and human action with full confidence, theologically speaking. Adaptation, on the same logic, where a created cultural good is taken up in another form, bespeaks the same confidence and lack of anxiety about breaking sacred limits. Rather, adaptation takes it that fidelity is oriented not only backwards to its source, but vertically before God, and also forwards to the day of judgment when works will be tested through fire. For now, in this framing, comics or graphic novels of the Pilgrimverse stand under theological judgment no more nor less than the "original" text. They can all point to the complex truth of what it means to be human before God, and only then, to the standard of faithfulness to the original text. Yet, given the clear communicative task of these works to theological truth of the gospel in line with the original, to the extent that they are then not only illustrative but instructive, the weight of their prophetic Christian instruction through aesthetic style, transformation, correction, omission of elements of Bunyan's text will be subject to proleptic prophetic judgment.

FAI: Hold on! Proleptic?!

RES: Sorry, I was on a roll there, nerdwise. Proleptic means anticipatory, or being offered in advance of the main event. So proleptic judgment is the discernment, in this case, that Christians and others might be invited to exercise in anticipation and ultimate deference to God's last judgment on all things.

FAI: Thanks.

RES: You're welcome. In short, theology can weigh in among other perspectives with preliminary and participative rather than final judgments about faithfulness. Another way of saying this is that once an adaptation is ventured in the Pilgrimverse it is drawn into a world of religious significance, and often aimed at a religious marketplace where form and content ought to be judged together. The goodness of the artist's craft is tied to, but not subordinate to the goodness of the message told by the art. . . . Um, guys?

    I saw in my dream that Faithful and Hopeful had sat down while Researcher had been speaking. Their eyes seeming a little glazed and heavy as he reached his conclusion. It took a few more coughs and prompting calls to regain their attention.

FAI: Sorry about that, our scouting expedition was tiringly thrilling.

HOP: Yeah, pretty action-packed stuff, all those versions of the same battle.

RES: Hmnn, ok, enough theory, back to the action. How do the graphic novels do in conveying this encounter as spiritual battle? After all, it turns out that this encounter is a perfect text of adaptation, because the fighting is only a brief element of Bunyan's attention in the text compared to his emphasis on dialogue. And that dialogue is all about Apollyon's claim over Christian as Lord of the City of Destruction. It's about Christian's defiance in sticking to the King's Highway even though he has been a failure in his journey. And about God's faithfulness to forgive notwithstanding. Very significant is the way Christian's sword, as the sword of the Spirit of Ephesians 6, is a transformed version of his book and his scroll, that is, as the Bible; and how this is conveyed visually.

FAI: Good point. Bunyan is very careful to prefix Christian's victory moment with the providential "But as God would have it." And only then does Christian manage to pick up his fallen sword.

HOP: And it is actually with words that it seems he strikes his enemy, saying, first, "Rejoice not against me, O mine enemy: when I fall, I shall arise," which is from Micah 7:8. This is described as a "deadly thrust," which gives Apollyon a "mortal wound."

FAI: Right, but he doesn't die, so Christian "made at him again, saying," that is, without even making an allegorical reference to the physical sword, and only using words . . .

HOP: (interrupting) And "Apollyon spread forth his dragon's wings, and sped him away"!

FAI: Wait, it's the words that matter: Christian says, "Nay, in all these things we are more than conquerors, through him that loved us." Straight out of Romans 8:37. The him being God in Jesus Christ.

RES: And don't you love how Bunyan weaves in the allusion to Revelation, the book that brings Bible readers to the Celestial City in its final chapters? When he writes of Apollyon's mortal wound which is based on the wound in the head of the beast that comes from the dragon in Revelation 13:3, 12, and 14.

HOP: Yeah, ok, that's a bit too nerdy for us, but we'll take your word for it. Bunyan does, however, give us the marginal references to Micah, Romans, and James 4:7 which says "Resist the Devil, he will flee from you." And Apollyon does indeed flee.

RES: So how do the graphic novels handle that theological claim of this as a spiritual battle?

FAI: We've seen that Vossos is thoroughly word-focused in this volume of his graphic novel. There is visual movement across panels to suggest the battle, but the pages are hand-written reproductions of the original text. Vossos gives us the words but not the explicit extratextual pointer to the

Bible to accompany Christian's conquering exclamations. He doesn't give the marginal references that Bunyan does. This is significant as a genre decision. Given that the guttering of the page is not the same as textblock margins, perhaps Vossos decides that footnotes don't belong in graphic novel text panels.

HOP: Still, you can't get much more faithful than giving the full text. How does the next novel fare?

I saw that Faithful, who'd been looking at Vossos's images, was surprised at the sound of Hopeful's voice. He looked across to where Hopeful had been but instead of seeing the companion he was used to, he saw instead a young woman, with brown hair.

FAI: Is that you, Hopeful?

HOP: Yes, and you'd better get used to the changes 'cos there are more coming up. I know neither of us are in the story yet at Christian's battle with Apollyon, but it seems the dynamics of exposure to these comics is affecting my self-presentation.

FAI: Evidently. So, this is you from . . . ?

HOP: From Lee Tung and Johnny Wong's Manga version. Tung and Wong convey the spirituality of the battle by interspersing the movement dynamics with vision sequences where Christian recalls his failures of the journey. He then sees the beast transform into a "very beautiful woman" indicating, no doubt, Satan's power of temptation. To be honest I'm not sure that's a fair portrayal of women for a spiritual classic.

FAI: Well, you've certainly got another perspective now. What else happens?

HOP: The nature of the sword is explicitly shown in a text box accompanying the fight sequence, saying "Sword of the Spirit." The following action box shows Christian "swooshing" his sword in the air with bird-like cloud-forms around him: the text in the panel reads, "Christian drew his sword. Some doves, symbols of the Holy Spirit, appeared as he waved the Sword." These doves then grapple with the fearsome beast. Some pages further on, as Apollyon and many demonic forces surround Christian, he, with sword set in the ground speak the words Bunyan originally used from Micah 7:8 and Romans 8:37, but Tung and Wong, like Vossos, don't add the explicit Bible references.

FAI: Christian shouts the verses out while holding above his head a large open book that he has pulled from his satchel. It is the Bible he was reading at the opening of the graphic novel. Holding it aloft invites a downward shaft of golden light from heaven which turns into a descending army of winged angelic warriors who do battle against the arraigned foes. Crying "resist the devil," that we recognize from James, a text box describes the image as "Christian gave Apollyon a deadly thrust with his Sword."

FAI: Al Bohl's battle is the most succinct, and with least dialogue. No Bible verses are quoted or referred to in his comic. But when it comes to spiritual content, we are told in narrative text boxes that "Christian fought valiantly with a strength not his own." However, less spiritually, the tactical thrust that repelled the creature came about because "Finally Apollyon let down his guard at the wrong time." For the purposes of the quick moving narrative, it is Christian's swordsmanship that wins the day. Yet there is more detail that emerges as Bohl's adaptation progresses.

RES: Like what?

FAI: Well, Bohl found an ingenious way to recreate a theological truth and overcome a big difficulty for the coherence of a visually driven rendition of Part I. Desperate to escape Doubting Castle, some pages on in the comic, Christian suddenly realizes: "My sword's handle looks like the key that hangs around the Giant's neck." And it does! Ever since he was given the sword in the Palace Beautiful, the entire hilt has been in the curious shape of a key! And now, not only does this solve a visual challenge of accounting for where Christian's key comes from in Doubting Castle . . .

HOP: (interrupting) Which Bunyan would be fine with because his metaphors are mixing all the time, anyway!

FAI: Right, the fact that Bunyan calls that key Promise tell us it is here again the word of God, the Bible, as the Sword of the Spirit.

HOP: So, you're saying, Bohl has his spiritual meaning covered with the Sword-as-Key-as-Promise plan. Nice!

    Faithful looked across to where Hopeful had been. But now he saw, instead of a young brown-haired woman, a chisel-jawed Asian man.

HOP: Choi's graphic novel was only assessable by us with images, and not words. But, it is clear that he gives Christian the same Bible verses to speak. The explicit references conclude the relevant speech bubbles in Arabic numbers, 7:8, 8:37, and 4:7. Notably, although the thrust of combat lasts some twenty-three panels over five pages, a battle of words in confrontation had already occupied eleven pages. And like Bunyan's text, Christian made at Apollyon after the first strike but, in the respective panel, it is his charge that is shown as he speaks out Romans 8:37. And the following panel shows Apollyon fleeing without another blow landing. The same was also communicated in Vossos's handling. This drawing of the battle's climax points to a work of spiritual victory rather than purely physical overcoming.

Faithful, again hearing Hopeful's voice change, looked across to where Hopeful had been. But instead of seeing the Asian man he had just become, now he saw instead, a burly black man.

FAI: I want to note a faithfulness issue here. (And I'm partly thinking this because your muscles are kind of bulging in my face all of a sudden, Hopeful.) Anyway, remember we spotted that Christian on Marvel's cover was substantially more pumped and uncovered than in the internal battle scenes?

HOP: Yes. Go on.

FAI: Well, unlike on the cover, in a telling detail of fidelity, Christian's breastplate does not spread round as armor for his back inside the comic.

HOP: Good catch. Both Tung & Wong and Choi had full body armor.

FAI: It is clear among these Marvel combat scenes that this is also a war of allegiances expressed in words—to Apollyon prince of the City of Destruction or to the King of Kings on whose road Christian has already traveled too far. The final panels show that it is Christian's lack of fear in making the conquering sword thrust deep into the beast's chest that ends the battle, but arguably his lack of fear is premised on the preceding exchange: Apollyon says, "Fool. Your God died on the cross." This verbal charge provokes a rebuttal from Christian, as he resists being pulled by a serpentine tongue into the open-mouthed-belly of the beast: ". . . when he died on the cross, he also rose again!" Although not explicit, this is the creative moment where the novel's script evokes a resurrection reading of Micah 7:8 in line with the hope of Romans 8:37.

HOP: I like your read. It appears less overtly biblical and spiritual, but still focuses a reader on the gospel by pointing to Jesus' overcoming of death.

FAI: Yeah, like a case of creative gospel fidelity conformed to the genre and its purposes for the collaboration of publishers.

Again in my dream I saw that Faithful looked across to where Hopeful had been. But instead of seeing the black man, a dreadlock-wearing black woman stood her ground.

FAI: Is this making you dizzy?

HOP: Interestingly, each time I change I still feel fully me—must be consistent within-story writing.

FAI: So this time you're from?

HOP: Stephen Moore's more autobiographically framed novel. Did you know he used his own friends as models for his drawing of his characters? Pretty cool, right?

FAI: I guess. How does he do?

HOP: Moore has an Apollyon who first appears as a false king figure and then transforms into a dragon beast. There are a couple of pages of silent fight action, but most of this encounter is a dialogue clash of allegiances, such as Bunyan portrays. The battle ends with a thrust to the hilt of Christian's sword, as he says "My sin was erased by the death of Christ. He conquered death. You—the accuser- Lord of the flies, you have no power over me . . . be gone in Jesus' name!" The thought bubble that accompanies Apollyon's departure reads, "What would have been a mortal blow, if I fought flesh and blood, came by speaking the Word of God—His promise to me [. . .] now I know how to win." Moore has his autobiographical pilgrim explicitly explain the encounter theologically as spiritual, evoking the armor of God passage from Ephesians 6:11–18 where the battle is not "against flesh and blood," and that the artist had quoted in full, with the reference, in a text box as Christian was being dressed earlier in Palace Beautiful's armory. Tellingly, the sword in the armory is pictured glowing, as it hovers over an open Bible, keeping the "Sword of the Spirit: the Word of God" reference to the fore.

FAI: Nice visual touch there. So, the spirituality of the sword as tied to God's word has been established visually beyond the directions Bunyan had given in his text?

HOP: Yes, but in creative support of the same communication. Now, moving on from these Christianly attuned adaptations, we should turn to Ralph Sanders's *Pilgrim's Progress*. I've had a quick browse, and neither of us is in it. I'm really not sure it's going to be your cup of tea.

FAI: You don't think an adaptation set in a modern dystopia in black and white scratchboard style with a solo pilgrim on a motorbike is going to push my faithful adaptation buttons? Well, I guess you have a point. So, who's going to take over?

HOP: Let's hand this one over to Researcher. He ought to do some work, and I could do with a rest from all those metamorphoses.

RES: OK, guys, I'll take over for Sanders's graphic novel. It's an interesting example, actually, of what fidelity can look like to a strand of Bunyan's vision when loosened from his religious hope in Christ. I think we could recognize that *The Pilgrim's Progress* ends up speaking of humane, secular values in an inspiring way to those who pay attention to it. Sanders is not opposed to Christianity like Atheist who you came across with Christian, Hopeful. His vision is, I think, oriented to a broadly liberal tolerance that is disgusted with selfish greed and violent intolerance in the present world. Sanders keeps mostly carefully to the chronology of Part I in depicting the motorcycle journey of his laptop-toting pilgrim. An example of his creative inclusiveness would be his depiction of an encounter with Evangelist as denoted by a marquee tent occupied by an Octopus creature whose tentacles each bear the symbol of a major religion or belief system. His book also ends with an interplanetary escape to a blissful ring of Saturn on the basis of "time well spent." It is a hope beyond, but not a spiritually Christian celestial one, of a rejection of late liberal militarism and consumerism that leads to soul satisfaction rather than oblivion.

FAI: And Apollyon?

RES: Oh, yes. I would kind have thought this would be a bigger part of the novel, but once a Worldly-Wiseman-besuited-owl creature drinking Faith Beer and touting heavy artillery has been encountered, the scathing critique of evil runs throughout and has no place for a crowning personification. Instead, intriguingly, Apollyon appears as text on the page that shows the pilgrim reaching the salvage yard by the King's Highway. There, with three angelic bikers in pursuit, he finds a pile of scrap vehicles which is teetering high over the ground. The gaps between the cars mark the outline of a cross, portrayed, as it were, in its absence.

HOP: Those would be Bunyan's three shining ones who meet Christian when his burden falls off at the cross, right?

RES: Yes. And this is where Sanders's pilgrim drops the laptop bag, labeled burdens, that he has been carrying over his shoulder. He does so at the door of the "Apollyon Burden Drop." The illuminated sign "SIN" suggests this is where you bring these to be dropped, if sin is associated with the drop bins for needles and syringes, bottle, guns, money, and even family. There is a snake slithering below the sign that says "NO. TERROR." Maybe this is a warning not to go further with sin and destruction because all it holds out is terror.

HOP: Huh?

FAI: So, is this spiritual battle or not?

RES: My sense is that Sanders is definitely promoting an ethical wisdom that flees entrapment in the world's violence, hedonism, and commercialism. This could certainly be a secular spirituality, if that makes sense?

HOP: It is interesting to me that his visual style of scratch board etching is thoroughly modern in setting but old in terms of technique and texture.

FAI: Yeah, it does put it with Vossos on the visual faithfulness to Bunyan's original woodcut illustrations, even if the interpretation is very different.

NAR: Well, thanks, guys. I'm sure there are a wealth of details we could draw from these graphic novels, but we should probably get ready to move on. I'm responsible for the length of these chapters when your conversations are written up, you know. Researcher, can you bring some of these strands together?

RES: I think that it is futile, on the face of it, to bring a charge of iconoclasm against graphic novels. Yet if that which makes *The Pilgrim's Progress* a classic of Protestant spirituality is precisely its devotion to the Word of the Bible and Christ, some will judge faithfulness in adaptation in relation to this Word-ness. So, there is something distinctive in Vossos's dedication in preserving every word of the original within his adaptation. His art thus functions as an adornment for the text he reveres. *The Pilgrim's Progress*'s classic status is kept as pristine as possible in this curating, making Bunyan's text iconic in significant ways. This is an illustrated manuscript, but precisely in being so, it adapts the book to a visual mode of communication. Bunyan certainly wanted to guide his readers to correct interpretation, and his dreaming narrator plays that role. So, it's worth noting that Vossos incorporates the dreaming narrator into his panels.

NAR: I do like that!

FAI: That's a good spot.

HOP: What about the faithfulness of other adaptations?

RES: Choi, certainly, as well as Tung and Wong, keep all the original incidents of Bunyan's narrative in their adaptation. Marvel and Bohl produce slimmer comics so necessarily economize to reproduce the action of the journey rather than the encounters that are merely conversational. This means the big picture of salvation and perseverance through trials of faith is upheld. At the same time, details about avoiding hypocrisy, legalism, or license in holding out a Protestant articulation of atonement and justification by grace through faith are let go. All the same, because produced with religious intent, these along with Moore, all communicate an adherence to the piety that Bunyan sought to propagate.

HOP: So they're all different but in the same ball park of creatively adapting while aiming for faithfulness?

RES: I reckon an adaptation trajectory or spectrum in relation to the text would have Vossos at the nearest point on the left proximate to the original for language, followed by Choi, and the Tung and Wong, and then Moore, to Bohl, Marvel, and then Sanders over at the other end.

FAI: But something grabbed you about Sanders's work, didn't it?

RES: Yes, although as a theologian I read it as dismissing a Bunyanesque religious Protestant Christian vision in favor of a kind of progressive enlightenment. But what it does do, is it invites consideration of the decisions involved in adaptation where the graphic novel is a contemporary medium that also calls for faithfulness to the present concerns of readership. It is worth pointing out that those graphic novels whose intent is to explicitly maintain faithfulness to Bunyan's spirituality through use of Scripture and confessional dialogue are equally those whose visual setting and costuming place the story, for Vossos, Tung and Wong, and Bohl in the visual historical past, or for Moore in the fantasy past. There is a certain irony here given the contemporaneity of Bunyan's textual imagery in his very present seventeenth-century dissenting context. Now experienced as "ye olde" English, Bunyan's phrasing is the common speech of lower classes.

HOP: We should confess that we haven't been entirely fulsome in our reporting.

RES: How so?

HOP: We came across so many Korean graphic novels from the last three decades that we've ended up merely scratching the surface. Visually these run the gamut from medieval costuming to Choi's jeans clad pilgrims gaining armor, to teenagers and middle-aged office workers on pilgrimage.

RES: And for a different sense of scope, Tung and Wong's original Chinese Manga is now in English, French, and Portuguese.

HOP: Sorry, didn't meant to break your flow!

RES: No worries. Where was I?

FAI: Spirituality and doctrine are inextricably entwined in a Christian perspective?

RES: Indeed! Vossos, Bohl, Moore, Choi, and Tung and Wong all share Bunyan's essential theological convictions about the narrow way to salvation being faith confessed in Jesus Christ, whose death on the cross atones for human sin. Marvel, too, pays heed to the heroic suffering of Jesus on the cross which liberates Christian of his burden. But the place of Marvel in this dimension of the Pilgrimverse makes me wonder whether a genre given to hero exploits can capture and communicate the essential passivity of a Christian receiving welcome and forgiveness through no work of their own.

FAI: You mean that the expectation and framing of reading comics might bias the reader to misperceive pointers to divine grace as just further plot moments in an adventure of human achievement?

RES: Something like that, yes.

HOP: If anything, something of Bunyan's protagonist's passivity is kept by Sanders as Pilgrim just plugs away on his motorcycle journey, heading onward, ever onward.

FAI: Do any of these visual recontextualizations effectively rule out fidelity to Bunyan?

RES: To the extent that the adaptation evokes the affective impact of the original and strikes a chord with memories then it is an adaptation. But we need too, to consider that the graphic novel market is likely reaching readers by age or inclination who may not have read nor ever plan to read the original.

NAR: Picking up on the framing verse I'll use for this chapter, 3 John 5, the apostle addresses a friend, whose faithfulness is encouraging strangers they don't know. I take it that we've seen some of this going on in the reach of graphic novels, bringing the Pilgrimverse to readers who may not otherwise come across Bunyan.

RES, FAI and HOP: (together) Yes.

NAR: And we can agree that Christian readers ought to be theologically committed to seeing, hearing and diligently caring for expressions of human creativity, perhaps especially as these arise in intertextual conversation with a spiritual classic like *The Pilgrim's Progress*. So rather than defensiveness, appreciation is in order in this corner of the Pilgrimverse. Both Marvel and Sanders hit on key contemporary concerns in their highlighting environmental degradation and social isolation of cities. If Bunyan was exercised by both spiritual battle with Apollyon and the possibility of persecution when he wrote of Vanity Fair, there is no reason to suppose the some of the greater crises of our age cannot frame the spiritual significance of his work today. In fact, Sanders's blistering critique of late modern consumer capitalism may not be so far from the tinker's original vision. It is possible, then, to recognize that treating a "timeless" classic as either, with Vossos, Bohl and Tung and Wong, a clarion call from a godly past, or with Moore, an existential fantasy, might stand in line with spiritualizing readings of the book, but need not be the only way to adapt it faithfully and "timefully." A material and earthy hope emerging from the vernacular dialects and delightfully described social scene in Bunyan's original can support Moore's creative collaging which showcases mixed media materiality, Choi's visual interweaving of backdrops and characterization from Biblical narrative to modern cityscapes, or Sanders's relentlessly contemporary technological dystopia.

HOP: And I guess my own transformations through these graphic novels show artists aware of a diverse readership in a racially diverse society, different in extent to Bunyan's day. In Choi's version I end up with long hair in the comics' ending scenes, but this has been growing out from the shaven head I sport when joining Christian as a mark of my pre-conversion life as a Buddhist monk. Writing an adaptation of *The Pilgrim's Progress* in a Pilgrimverse that encompasses religious difference beyond the intra-Christian one of Catholic and Protestant calls for different representations of conversion.

FAI: And if, in the present social setting, the church that clings to Bunyan has awoken to its failings to attend, in love, to the lives, voices, and bodies of women and ethnic and racial minorities, some of your transformations evidence corrections.

HOP: I guess so.

RES: Even so, it's not so clear women are equal partners in the Pilgrimverse, perhaps as a legacy of Bunyan's original writing. You guys take a rest, because we're going to pursue this question some more as we survey the Pilgrimverse with a lens of Christian missionary outreach. And to do that well we are going to need to climb to the highest peak. Sorry.

NAR: Take a rest, guys. We don't need to begin that journey today.

Pilgrimverse Resources:

Bohl, Al. *The Pilgrim's Progress.* New Barbour Christian Comics. Uhrichsville, OH: Barbour & Company, 1994.
Choi, Chol-Kyo. *The Pilgrim's Progress.* 3 vols. Seoul, S. Korea: Word of Life, 2019.
Powell, Martin, et al. *The Pilgrim's Progress.* Marvel Comics: The Christian Classics Series. New York: Marvel Entertainment Group, 1992.
Moore, Stephen T. *The Pilgrim's Progress.* CreateSpace Independent Publishing Platform, 2011.
Sanders, Ralph. *Pilgrim's Progress. The Graphic Novel.* Santa Cruz, CA: Whistle Key, 2018.
Tung L. and Wong J. *The Pilgrim's Progress.* Vols. 1–2. Leesburg, FL: Kingstone Comics, 2011.
Vossos, Steve. *The Pilgrim's Progress.* Vols. 1–3. Kelowna, BC: BooInk, 2017–19.

Further Reading with Mr Researcher:

Draycott, Andy. "Iconoclasm, Iconophobia, and Graphic Novel Adaptations of John Bunyan's *The Pilgrim's Progress." Journal of Graphic Novels and Comics* 12:5 (2021) 964–92.

4

Church

> Light in a messenger's eyes brings joy to the heart,
> and good news gives health to the bones.
>
> PROVERBS 15:30

In my dream, Researcher came into his office, removed and hung up his coat, and then looked around his desk at the arrayed artefacts of the Pilgrimverse. After a while he sat down, as if to wait. He was reaching for one of the books when Faithful and Hopeful rounded the side of a particularly large pile and greeted him.

RES: Hi, guys. I know that graphic novel dimension might have seemed to be an obscure and at the same time dangerous corner of the Pilgrimverse. But now I can promise you guys a more familiar scene.

HOP: Uh oh, are you gonna send us back into our book without any further adventures?

RES: No, no, nothing like that, yet. There's plenty more of the Pilgrimverse to map. What I mean is that we're going to church. I want to get a sense for how *The Pilgrim's Progress* has featured in church life, in its presentation to Christians, and as a tool to present Christianity to non-Christians.

FAI: So, like a ministry and missions perspective?

Researcher reached for a small aging booklet in hard binding no bigger than his palm.

RES: Yes, let me give you a historical example from the late nineteenth century that I came across. It's called *The Probationer's Companion*.

HOP: What's a "probationer"?

RES: A "probationer" is someone who is being proved as a new follower of Jesus. So, in the instance of this booklet it means a new Christian confirming their faith in the gathering of an American Methodist Episcopal church. My copy has a certificate page at the beginning where a handwritten entry indicates that it belonged Eva Hurlbut of the Roxbury, Connecticut, church in the New York East Conference, and her pastor was George Bennet, Jr.

FAI: Are they famous?

RES: What? No, that's not the point. Rather, the opposite. We get a glimpse into ordinary lives around the Pilgrimverse here. The beginning of her probation is dated as of March 21, 1897. The Companion booklet starts by explaining that Probation is a firm commitment envisioning eventual reception into church membership. The daily disciplines or duties of Bible reading and secret prayer are the mainstays of the probationer's life. The history and organizational structure of the church is set out.

FAI: That's pretty full on!

RES: Well, there's more, which is why this is in the Pilgrimverse.

HOP: OK, go on.

RES: All this must mean that Eva was showing interest in the Christian faith and was prepared to learn more about belief and Christian living as preparation for a full commitment, apparently, in her case, through baptism. I say apparently, because the page of the *Companion* after the probation entry certificate shows another certificate indicating that Eva was received into membership upon her baptism on March 27, 1898. What's significant for the Pilgrimverse is that the *Companion* booklet actually ends with a summary of *The Pilgrim's Progress* Part I. Effectively this is a set of compressed notes guiding a reader through the story.

HOP: That's pretty cool. So, she'd have met me, as it were?

RES: Well, in fact, there's no way of knowing if Eva used the terse summary notes to accompany an actual reading of the book, or just read the

Into the Pilgrimverse

notes, or whether her probation period was used to read at all. But it is significant that over two hundred years after its publication, on another continent, John Bunyan's book is not just thought of as a classic but is recommended to new Christians for their edification and instruction.

Faithful reached out his hand and touched the booklet Researcher was holding and received a little jolt upon contact that send a shiver over his body.

HOP: What was that?

FAI: Well, I reckon that our last journey into the Pilgrimverse has a lasting impact. Just touching this book has given me a "memory" of its contents as if by a kind of download. Maybe this pilgrimnaut gig will get easier?

HOP: "Pilgrimnaut"! Really? Are you expecting me to use that word?

FAI: What? While we go about our pilgrimnavigation? Sure! No?

HOP: No!

FAI: Oh, all right. Anyway, fun fact about this *Pilgrim's Progress* summary: Ignorance is a dude!

HOP: We all know that Ignorance was male, what's your point?

FAI: What I mean is that the pastor, Rev. J. O. Peck, DD, who writes the summaries of *The Pilgrim's Progress* in note form uses the word "dude" to introduce Ignorance. The word wasn't in use before 1877, so this is a pretty early attestation of a term now more commonly found on the lips of California surfers. Pretty gnarly, right?

Hopeful, impressed, leans backwards against another book from the same pile Researcher had taken the *Companion* from. This one, by contrast, is a twenty-first-century paperback. Receiving the same jolt, he laughs at the sensation, then says:

HOP: Well, I don't know about Eva, but it seems like Adam is in view with this book. It's a ministry primer for men who need bolstering in their faith in a world of toxic masculinity and emasculating cultural chic. Well, that's my paraphrase. Here's what the author, Joe Barnard has to say: "In the English-speaking world (the part I know) men are languishing, and in desperate need of spiritual counsel.[. . .] This book is for stage two-Christians [. . .] men, who know the gospel, who profess, faith, who, long for transformation, but who are frustrated by the lack of spiritual growth."

FAI: And what's that got to do with the Pilgrimverse?

HOP: Well, the first whole book Joe Barnard recommends for getting men kick-started on their reinvigorated path of Christian discipleship is *The Pilgrim's Progress*. He writes: "Once men have a foundational understanding of the gospel and the doctrines of grace, they then need to develop a true perspective on the nature of the Christian life as a whole. There is no better way of doing this than reading John Bunyan's classic, *Pilgrim's Progress*." And Barnard's *Cross-Training Ministry* has a dedicated website with videos and podcasts, so it's thoroughly up to date.

FAI: So, Researcher, can we just climb up and jump right in? Same kind of need as before, survey, describe and analyze what we find, right?

RES: Go for it!

From seemingly out of nowhere there comes a shout of "Hold on a minute there, boys!" Researcher, Faithful and Hopeful look around to see who was interrupting and they see, emerging from behind a rather clunky CD player, two figures, marching toward them at some pace.

The shout, repeated, if anything, a little louder still than the first time, "I said, hold on a minute there, boys!" came from the slightly taller of the pair. She was instantly recognizable from Part II, or even from the short glimpses given in Part I. It was Christiana.

FAI: Hello, Christiana, fancy meeting you here? I mean, technically, we've never met, or at least, not textually speaking. And I assume this is Mercy with you?

Christiana: That's right, we're pretty much a twosome, for the purposes of pilgrimaging.

HOP: So what pilgrimaging are you up to, right now?

CNA: Well, that's just it. We heard about this Pilgrimverse exploration. Hello, Mr Researcher.

RES: Hello.

CNA: And getting wind of the work, we thought we'd better break up the boys-only club feel of this expedition before it's too late.

HOP: Well, if you recall, the last expedition report had me cast as two different female Hopefuls.

Mercy: In fairness, that's not what we mean. We're going to take over this one from here. You are stood down. Is that all right, Mr Researcher?

RES: Just Researcher is fine. No need for the Mr.

CNA: Well, Mr. does rather make our point.

RES: Which is?

CNA: That the pilgrimverse expeditions deserve to have some female representation as we take the helm in half of the text.

FAI: Well, actually . . .

MER: That'll do, Faithful. Are you going to tell us we only made if because Great-heart guided us? Are you?
Faithful read the room well enough to stay silent . . .

MER: Because, incidentally, it's by the same grace of God that brings Christian to his journey's end that the same is done for us.

RES: And the Pilgrimverse has always been well served by women writers, scholars and artists, it's true. From the membership of the International John Bunyan Society, the pages of the Bunyan Studies academic journal, editors and contributors to Oxford Handbook and Cambridge Companions, to children's adaptations, contemporary re-tellings, and devotional surveys and studies, this is by no means a men-only field. So, by all means, go ahead.

CNA: We were going anyway, but thanks, we're glad to help.
With that Faithful and Hopeful backed away to sit down on the desk and Christiana and Mercy opened the *Companion* booklet the Researcher had put down on the desk, and entered the Pilgrimverse portal by way of Eva Hurlbut's certificate of the completion of her probation.
Some while later, I saw in my dream that the two women explorers emerged from the same portal into which they'd disappeared.

CNA: OK, we found a ton of things, but there's also a whole expanse of the Pilgrimverse that we could travel around but with little understanding.

RES: Faithful and Hopeful seem to have sloped off. Why don't you let me and the Narrator hear what you found.

MER: OK, for starters: Did you guys know that *The Pilgrim's Progress* has been translated into more than 200 languages? Most of those translations were done by Protestant missionaries.

CNA: Yeah. It turns out that after the New Testament, *The Pilgrim's Progress* is a lot quicker to translate than the whole of the Old Testament, so that Bunyan was often slotted into translation programs in that order.

MER: And even beyond the spiritual conversation the translations opened up for the missionaries, the very act of translation into local languages of a non-Scriptural text also ended up having the impact of empowering secular literary traditions outside of colonial languages. Such is the case documented in relation to Tiyo Soga's 1868 Xhosa translation in South Africa or modern Korean with William Gale's 1895 translation.

CNA: I feel we have to point out that missionary translation doesn't have to mean there is popular demand or subsequent avid readership. The cases of pages of Bunyan's text being used to wrap fresh fruit and vegetables in Hawaii, or the book being used as an English primer for native Americans in jail who needed the colonial tongue to defend themselves in court stand out as less than immediately spiritually transformative encounters with the book.

MER: The thing is, though, even with all this evidence of missionary translations, we still came out of our books in English.

CNA: We know from Bunyan's preface to Part II that his Part I was already traveling to difference countries within a few years of publication. At the same time, Bunyan is used to this day as an introduction to English literature and culture. So, we spotted a 2020 edition of *The Pilgrim's Progress* from the Liaoning People's Publishing House, China, that was packaged as a bedside classic for students. The Preface was first in English then, it seemed, in Chinese, with an Introduction also in Chinese. And we read about tens of different translations of *The Pilgrim's Progress* into Chinese over the nearly two centuries since its first appearance from William Chalmers Burns in 1853. The resurgence in recent years since the opening up of China for the twenty-first century has seen a proliferation of both secular, academic editions and explicitly, religious, evangelistic editions.

MER: The challenge of culture and translation might be well illustrated by our discussing not a book, but a movie, don't you think, Christiana?

CNA: You mean the 2019 Robert Fernandez directed, CGI animated, *Pilgrim's Progress* movie?

MER: Yes. It's produced by Revelation Media, a not-for-profit distribution ministry working on missionary projects from a US base. The ministry has translated the movie into over fifty languages.

CNA: Revelation Media's mission statement reads like this: "Produce and license culturally relevant and engaging media that leads people into a relationship with our Creator. Translate the media into the top languages of the World alongside global ministry partners. Distribute the media, making it freely available to the missionary!"

MER: That translation effort is, of course, a translation of the voice over track accompanying the animation. So, it is interesting to ask about translation of the visual cues, the visual humor, and even the ambient soundtrack. How do these shape reception of a movie without translation?

CNA: That's right. After all, for example, we've learned that in China, where *The Pilgrim's Progress* has been translated, Chinese illustrations have drawn Pilgrim's Progress into their own imaginative framework in relation to the image of the Gate. But this traditional imagination lies side by side with the global influence of specifically Western animation styles recognized by many and appreciated by the older generation in China. That earlier book we mentioned in the bedside classics series does have illustrations for its Chinese readers but these are classic late nineteenth-century English ones locating the book abroad rather than contextualizing it for home.

MER: So the answer must be complicated. For example, if the resonance of the stirring chorus of the hymn, Be Thou My Vision, provides an emotional setting for Christian's climb to the cross whereupon he is released of his burden, around the 48-minute mark, does this lose its impact where the hymn is unknown, or where music and the associated range of human emotions works in different beats? Or does the translation of words only exacerbate the colonization of sounds that replaces local musicking with Western international melodies? These are questions that cannot be answered generally, but they can be and should be asked.

CNA: The movie has fun touches. The celebrity voice acting of John Rhys-Davies as Evangelist connects the visual dream fantasy of Bunyan to the cinematic success of Peter Jackson's Lord of the Rings movie franchise, in which Rhys-Davies played the stout dwarf warrior Gimli. But, beyond the Anglophone world, however, again, the resonance will be lost unless the same dubbing artist happens to be employed, which is highly unlikely.

MER: Interestingly, and open to interpretation in a number of ways, the most prominent ideological theme of the movie that exaggerates Bunyan's concerns is that of family. As the culmination of that emphasis, the movie has Christian reluctant to cross the river of Death to the Celestial City because he wants to go back and save his family.

CNA: I appreciate the sentiment, but it's not in the book!

MER: Fair call. This very clear "family-values" emphasis is interestingly primarily individualist. The Western nuclear family, of individually contracted marriage, is in view—and potentially over against, rather than for, wider ties to society and a more collectivist familial understanding.

CNA: Researcher is looking concerned!

RES: Sorry, I didn't mean to. But I was wondering where you were going?

MER: As well you might, especially if you see the gospel of the church's mission and belonging as only concerned with an individual's spiritual fate.

RES: Well, I'm not sure I'd put it only like that . . .

CNA: Whatever. Let's maybe start again, at the most obvious point, the one pointed out by Joe Barnard. The fact is, even within the pages of the book, there Christian, Faithful, and Hopeful all narrate their own experiences of conversion. They point to the central truth of Jesus and his righteousness covering their sin, grace overcoming the demands of the law, so that a repentant sinner can then walk free in joy of assurance of God's love.

MER: And that's what we experienced as we approached the Wicket Gate ourselves in Part II. Particularly because I didn't think myself worthy of or even invited on pilgrimage, my reception through the gate was evidence of a welcome for all.

CNA: So, we might say that, evangelistically, *The Pilgrim's Progress* functions as a story full of testimony of divine grace at work in people's lives. These life stories are offered as evidence of the power of the gospel. You can imagine this kind of story as part of one-on-one conversation about what it means to become a Christian, just as it could occur as the star turn at an evangelistic outreach event.

MER: In fact, that's how the story of Part I functions in the recording of BreakNTruth's breakdance ministry performance, where the YouTube video of the performance of Pilgrim's Progress is interrupted and tail-ended by testimony that invites viewers to know Jesus.

CNA: In this it is actually echoing the books, as they are chock of telllings and retellings of accounts of conversion and the experience of Salvation.

In fact, I had to laugh that my Christian was so typical in going on about his conversion so many times along his journey.

MER: But not typical as self-centered or boastful?

CNA: No, that might be how it could be read today. But, no, in fact there's a continual humbling in acknowledging the need for salvation from outside your own resources, so that sharing that testimony is to the praise of God's faithfulness.

MER: Right, so church families in Bunyan's day would hear testimony to check out someone's credentials for membership and then also to worship together.

CNA: As remains true in many church settings through to today.

MER: Of course. And that praise is both an inward encouraging of already believers kind of thing, as well as a missionary witness to those who do not acknowledge Jesus as their Lord, isn't that so, Christiana?

CNA: Certainly, we must suppose that the consistent use of *The Pilgrim's Progress* by missionaries in translation is a response to its usefulness as a means to sharing the good news of Jesus. Here's one such testimony: Robert Scott Oyebode tells that he received the text of *Pilgrim's Progress* in English, along with an English dictionary, in West Africa in the late nineteenth century. Oyebode writes of *Pilgrim's Progress* that "I am glad to say that I went through the book with great benefit to my soul; it first gave me an enlightenment as to what a true Christian life is, and from that time I can date my conversion."

MER: So we don't need to assume he'd never heard of Christianity or seen or read the Bible, but *Pilgrim's Progress* became the catalyst of his conversion.

CNA: Yes. In fact, it might be safer to assume Oyebode had heard the Christian gospel in some form or other, because, for a book used in Christian mission, it's surprising how little Bunyan in Part I explains the person and work of Jesus Christ.

MER: The integral dynamic of the biblical gospel, including the actual events of Jesus' life and ministry in the Gospels, is assumed rather than spelled out.

CNA: Yes. This, it appears, is a book addressed to the "race of saints" who are already embarked on their journey. It preaches pastoral encouragement for persevering pilgrims. Yet, already by the time of Part II, where our journey is offered as a "key" to the correct understanding of Part I, you find material included that is far more instructive on the shape of the gospel that animates the work.

MER: Remind me.

CNA: The cross is now visible from the wicket gate, and at the cross, Great-Heart delivers a lecture on Christology and Jesus' nature as God and Man. He goes on at great length explaining how Jesus' righteousness stands for sinners.

RES: And that's particularly handy given that Jesus is the righteous one whose righteousness was asserted in discourses on justification by faith in Part I, to Talkative and Ignorance, for example.

CNA: Quite so. Our Part II is doctrinally dense, wouldn't you say, Mercy?

MER: Oh yes, we love testing each other's knowledge of key teachings, from the kids on up. And we're denser on the road, too, aren't we?

CNA: Oh, you mean there are more of us in the company of pilgrims. Yes, that's certainly true. Part II ends up having a whole host of us on the road. And I actually think that has an impact on the way Bunyan intends the gospel to be understood.

MER: Not only do I get to do my thing, you know, the acts of mercy for the poor, but also the church community gets to act in solidarity with the society around it in impressive ways.

CNA: That's right, like when Great-heart leads the company of men out of Vanity to defeat the child-slaying Monster.

MER: So, the gospel compels neighborly love and care for the vulnerable.

CNA: Exactly, and even though the fighting is left to the men, we may as well note that Bunyan gives Gaius a long speech in praise of women and their place in the biblical and gospel narratives, and so also in the church.

MER: Even if Bunyan's still pretty traditional in his portrayal of us women, in fact.

CNA: Yes, it's a curious thing to see advocacy in his setting while assuming the need of male guidance and protection.

MER: But is it so curious? Sadly, our sex's vulnerability is a fact of life in the seventeenth century, without police forces or inheritances for social or economic security, but the truth is, this remains a consideration, despite some progress, through to this day.

CNA: Yes, sadly the attempted rape we suffer early in our journey in Part II only mirrors the reality of gender violence we continue to see today.

MER: But an emphasis only on Part I in missionary usage in the Pilgrimverse can obscure the social kingdom dimensions of the gospel. Do you remember getting that sense, Christiana?

CNA: I do. Yes. I would say, having thought about this, that the gospel is rarefied by being articulated in terms of the doctrines of justification which explain the impact of salvation on the individual. But this can end up ignoring the story of God's action in history through Israel and her Messiah. So, Christ's incarnation and kingdom ministry gets split from the proclamation of the atoning achievements of his coming.

MER: Jesus' cross, resurrection, and glorious ascension, and his second coming that is anticipated in the empowering of presence of the Holy Spirit is not solely about individual rescue but the formation of a people with a calling and mandate?

CNA: Yes, and it's there in Part I, in the Palace Beautiful or the Delectable Mountains and even Beulah land, but the journey tends to win out as it focuses on the destination attained by a few only.

MER: And, to be clear, we love the destination!

CNA: Certainly. But, for example, in the evangelist J. John's adaptation of the book in support of his gospel proclaiming ministry, Vanity, as a place is reduced to the quick site of Faithful's martyrdom.

MER: Tell me more. Researcher should hear this in full. It gives a good sense of contemporary evangelical use of Bunyan for evangelism.

RES: I'm all ears.

CNA: OK, so, in his overview of his abridged version of the book John reveals the character of his own winsome evangelistic appeal. He summarizes in terms of the abiding and accompanying love of God, writing, "From the first scene onward, Bunyan affirms that human beings are not lonely captains of their destiny. Behind the lives of each character, another figure lovingly walks with them and is in fact the final destination itself. The Pilgrim's Progress tells tales of individuals on the road of life and the story of how a loving God constantly teaches, loves and draws people to himself. Every step of the way, God accompanies each person, revealing the way of salvation."

MER: Yes! I mean, he's right to speak out against loneliness, but the individualist orientation remains when the focus in on direct connection with God without those churchly elements of fellowship that the book witnesses to, and presumes in its original, gathered, dissenting Christian readership.

CNA: Right, in other words, just when John might have sounded the churchly notes of Christian's fellowship with Evangelist, who guides him along the way, with companions Faithful and then Hopeful, and with the gathered family of the Palace Beautiful and the shepherds of the Delectable mountains, the individual seeker is given direct access to God but little notice of the gathered saints of the kingdom to accompany them.

MER: We're still talking "John" about J. John, as in the evangelist's last name, and not John Bunyan, the author's first name, correct?

CNA: Yes, definitely worth being clear on that!

RES: Ok. I'm tracking. Carry on.

CNA: To be clear, in many ways, John is faithful to not alter Bunyan's convictions. He keeps references to divine wrath, the burden of conviction of sin, and he does not smooth over the repeated failures of Christian to be Christian.

RES: So, the text that remains through abridgement speaks of the same gospel?

CNA: Quite, but maybe also, almost?

MER: Expand that a little, sister?

CNA: A change of register is particularly to be noted in John's treatment of the Vanity Fair episodes from both Parts I and Parts II. These are well known as the sites of Bunyan's clearest social critiques, aren't they?

RES: They are. From the cultural form of the Fair and its entertainments, to the legal and juridical culture, as well as an obviously religious critique—it's all in Vanity Fair.

CNA: Exactly. So remember that, as Bunyan relates his authorial dream, Christian and Faithful, having been warned by Evangelist, arrive at Vanity and immediately create a "hubbub" by their differences of clothing, of speech, and of comportment, refusing to buy the Fair's wares. They cry out that they will only buy the truth. Fights break out around them, they are arraigned, caged, and brought to trial.

MER: Faithful is eventually martyred, before Christian escapes.

CNA: And for Bunyan, this Part I episode takes up nine pages of text in modern full editions, compared to J. John's one-page rendering. With John, Faithful is still martyred but the reasons are left mysterious. All we are told "Now while they were there, Faithful and Christian were both imprisoned and brought to court." Faithful is found guilty, although we do not know of what, and sentenced to death. The gory details of his death, however, remain in the adaptation.

MER: And did you know that, aside from the illustrated frontispiece of the dreaming Bunyan, the first ever illustration of the narrative was the fourth edition's inclusion of a woodcut of Faithful burning at the stake.

CNA: This Vanity Fair episode is significant for a reading of Pilgrim's Progress, yet J. John down plays it. Why might J. John not consider this substantial abridgment a loss for his narrative? What does it tell us about his gospel? The answer, I suggest, has to do with the social aspects that for John are merely outcomes of the gospel rather than its kingdom core.

MER: The abridgment of the Vanity Fair episode, and particularly that trial scene removes the class-conscious critique, of the wealthy and aristocratic, and of the sycophantic aspirations to worldly status of the perjuring witnesses. Bunyan is very clear in his marginal notes that "Sins are all Lords and Great ones." An accuser reports Faithful and Christian's alleged "railing against" Price Beelzebub, Lord Old-man, Lord Carnal-Delight, Lord Luxurious, Lord Desire of Vain-glory, Lord Lechery, Sir Having greed and "the rest of our nobility."

CNA: Faithful denies the railing, but simply points out "the Prince of this Town, with all the Rablement his Attendants, by this Gentleman named, are more fit for a being in Hell, then in this Town and Countrey; and so the Lord have mercy on me."

MER: That the presiding magistrate is named Judge "Hategood" tells us that the institutions of human government and justice cannot be trusted with the truth and with life.

CNA: Bunyan's pilgrim gospel is one that turns the conventional and institutional confidences of the world upside-down.

MER: Social and political persecution are in Bunyan's view.

CNA: Now, I do not want to suggest that John presents an ethereal gospel of gnostic spirituality that is all comfortable metaphor. It could be that he deemed the communication of the core of the Christian gospel transformation wrought by salvation need not be encumbered by social critiques that are historically located in the past.

MER: At the same time, what difficulty there is envisaged for a follower of his twenty-first-century pilgrim way is primarily personal and private. It is a person's internal world of belief that is being challenged in evangelism, and only secondarily, as a possible consequence, their orientation to the social setting of discipleship.

CNA: If evangelism presents a gospel refracted through this abridgment of Pilgrim's Progress, it points to a mode of Christian discipleship marked by agency of decision and action. John's plot moves quickly. Bunyan's original is far more passive. The abridgments of the Vanity Fair episode in Part II illustrate this point even more.

RES: We don't often think of Part II in evangelistic contexts, so this should be interesting. I'm glad J John kept it in.

MER: Fair observation. Again, John keeps many of Bunyan's emphases that are more socially oriented to the mixed company of pilgrims that we were.

CNA: But, again, he makes cuts at Vanity: he cuts the public service that Great-heart and his company undertake. The valiant pilgrims rid the town of the troubling apocalyptic seven headed, ten horned serpent monster. Notably, the monster is wounded and forced to beat a retreat rather than killed outright.

MER: This means that the godly Christians, though few in number, are still, at certain seasons, committed to protecting the people of Vanity Fair from the monster's weakened assaults.

CNA: Right. Bunyan holds up, in this transformed Vanity of Part II, a representation of settled pilgrimage among an ungodly people. Christians positively serve the good of the city.

But John is less interested in conveying a gospel of social obligation and community participation.

RES: So, are you ladies suggesting that where Bunyan shows his Christian community as civically minded and engaging social action, an Evangelist's adaptation and its abridgments, ends up, shall we say, being more sectarian?

CNA: We think so, yes. It's an illustration of how a text for evangelism reflects bigger decisions that are made in connecting spiritual transformation and social transformation as gospel realities.

RES: Let me see if I've understood you. See if this works as a summary: J. John's evangelistic use of Pilgrim's Progress contextualizes through abridgement. What is lost is the gospel's social character calling disciples to gather in mutual fellowship and to testify in conduct that challenges entrenched structures of oppression and greed. What is emphasized is a dramatic journey whose individualistic pilgrim agency is brought to the fore.

MER: That's fair. And we don't think this is solely a one-off phenomena. It fits with a way of framing the gospel for decisionsitic evangelism that has shaped evangelicalism since at least the second great awakening under Charles Finney.

CNA: And I do just want to follow up on your comment about the greater emphasis always having fallen on Part I. While that may be true, there's evidence that the imbalance between the popularity of the parts may not always have been so pronounced as it has become through the twentieth and into the twenty-first centuries.

RES: Like what? I'm interested.

MER: We found that nineteenth-century American author, Harriet Beecher Stowe was brought up reading *The Pilgrim's Progress*. And what's interesting about her is that the two times she quotes word for word from Bunyan in *Uncle Tom's Cabin*, her most famous book, both instances are from the text of Part II.

CNA: And Stowe's book is certainly a plea for social activism.

MER: We reckon we could claim that this relatively high profile of Part II fits a cultural moment in America of Protestant evangelical social activism and ascendancy that has been eroding ever since. The Interpreter's illustration of the man raking muck while ignoring heavenly glory above him gets turned into the critical comment on the dubious journalistic tactics of the popular press which President Teddy Roosevelt names muck-raking.

CNA: Is it too much to claim that the perpetual popularity of Part I often read apart from Part II increasingly fuels a male-led social anxiety of withdrawal and culture war among some religious readers?

RES: I'm not sure how to comment on that, but I do know you also checked out ways that the Pilgrimverse accumulates resources to build up Christians in their discipleship apart from their missionary outreach. Do we learn more from those resources on these questions?

MER: Good point, and you're right, Mr Researcher. *The Pilgrim's Progress* has been used plenty in encouraging Christians to continue and deepen their own spiritual journey.

CNA: Here's a quote from Japan to prove the point. This is what Mr Akira Takimoto of All Japan Revival Mission has to say: "After I became a Christian, I had the opportunity to read the immortal classic, 'Pilgrim's Progress,' several times and was most deeply moved every time." The quote is supplied to blurb a short graphic novel by Masaka Sato. Takimoto says that Sato "has produced a wonderful, beautiful, easy-to-read comic version of this classic story. This is a wonderful book, showing salvation is found in Jesus Christ alone, so I pray people all over the world will read it."

MER: Evangelism and encouragement from a classic can go hand in hand.

RES: Indeed.

CNA: It's a feature of the Pilgrimverse that preachers would often take *The Pilgrim's Progress* as their text for extended series of meetings, and the practice carries through to today. You can find examples on YouTube or SermonAudio.com.

MER: It seems likely that the earliest commentary to appear alongside the text of *The Pilgrim's Progress* by preachers like John Newton, William Mason, George Burder, and Thomas Scott originates in preaching series. This is manifestly the case for collections of lectures in the nineteenth century by George Cheever, George Offor, Charles Spurgeon, and Charles Overton, for example. Scottish preacher, Alexander Whyte, develops a series of portraits of characters from Bunyan's book across two volumes that becomes a steady-seller.

CNA: All of which is to say that preachers saw *The Pilgrim's Progress* as edifying for Christians and not just captivating for non-believers.

MER: And this recognition is evident through to the twenty-first century in a continued production of Bible Study booklets, devotional reflections, and longer commentaries.

CNA: And, by the way, Mr Researcher, if this strikes you as odd, I mean, Bible Studies not devoted to a book of the Bible, rest assured that book club like appreciation of spiritual classics goes back to the early days of Reformation Protestant life.

MER: A useful reminder of why it is Bunyan would have thought it worth writing at all in the first place.

CNA: Nicely said. So, yes, the Pilgrimverse has a ton of older and newer edifying uses of *The Pilgrim's Progress* for Christian readers.

MER: And parallel to what we've already observed in missionary translation, emphases in commentary arise in tacit conversation with culture.

CNA: Cheryl Ford's *Discipleship Course* is built out of her earlier modernized English re-telling and a 365-day devotional. The course makes her interpretative lens most obvious. Writing from the US in the 2010s, Ford uses questions around the Vanity Fair episode to surface participant's experiences of broader cultural conflict, but her focus in doing so is genuinely Scripture.

MER: Her coursebook is structured according to the seventeen chapters into which her retelling of PP Part I was originally divided. Each chapter study is spread generously over eight to ten pages with spaces to take notes. In sidebars a number of features are repeated in each study: a "Progress Memory Verse," a "Progress Tip," a "Definition" of a term like "Watchfulness" or "Hypocrite," a "Key Pilgrim's Perspective," and a "Progress Quote from Another Pilgrim" such as Spurgeon or C. S. Lewis. Each study ends with "Scriptures for Further Reflection," spaces for separate notes unconnected to answering the set questions, and the Bible verses used in this chapter set out in full.

CNA: When it comes to Vanity Fair, in her chapter 9, Ford's study prompts are worded to invite disclosure of opposition. She writes that "[t]he pilgrims caused a commotion because they were different. Do Christians in present-day society cause a commotion, or are we largely ignored? Do you see attitudes changing? What kind of opposition do Christians face here and abroad?"

MER: It's in the suggested answer for leaders that more of Ford's own posture is indicated. Leaders are informed that "[s]ome cause a commotion by standing for truth and righteousness; many more do not. Persecution is rising in our land, and it is getting more difficult to sit on the fence as a cultural Christian. Biblical Christianity is under assault and so are its adherents. We see battles raging on many fronts, from theological to ideological to practical."

CNA: For all that Ford draws out culture clash elements, we see that one of her initial questions frames discipleship peaceably rather than antagonistically with this opening statement: "We should seek to be peacemakers in this world, but it is no easy task."

MER: And it is clear that the cost of discipleship is a key emphasis for Ford, not least by quoting Dietrich Bonhoeffer in a sidebar at the very top of the chapter. Her question 9 asks, "How does Evangelist's exhortation related to persecution counter the beliefs of some Christians about lives that are blessed?" Vanity Fair offers material riches and other enticements to build reputation in the world counter to the word of God. Ford leads readers away from a prosperity gospel in this question, and further underlines this in question 15, observing that "we should be careful that things don't own us but rather that we own them."

CNA: She offers Eugene Peterson's *The Message* translation of 1 John 2:15–17 as "A Helpful Exhortation" sidebar—"Love not the world. Don't love the world's ways. Don't love the world's goods. [. . .] The world as all its wanting, wanting, wanting is on the way out—[. . .]"

MER: And the chapter closes with another sidebar, "An appeal," alerting readers to the plight of the persecuted global and domestic church, and exhorting prayer.

RES: It seems to me that Ford is deeply invested in guiding the disciples through her course, steering them to discern Scripture rightly.

CNA: Yes, Ford's is the most fulsome of several Bible Study guides on the market today. And while it suggests possible answers, its open question format does not prescribe interpretation in the same way that commentary treatments tend to.

MER: Devotional treatments that meditate on smaller sections of the *Pilgrim's Progress* narrative tend to be more allusive.

RES: What do you mean by that?

MER: I mean that they don't dig into detailed exegesis of Bunyan's text, but rather use his phrasing or a theme to invite reflection and prayer, and draw on core theological affirmations. They share the assumptions of their eighteenth- and nineteenth-century predecessors that Bunyan's work offers spiritual nourishment, but unlike their Victorian forebears they use participative rhetoric that is invitational.

CNA: Right, you mean in contrast to those preaching commentators who tend to strike a more paternalistic tone in conscripting the "dear reader," often with an exclamatory, "O!" into lamenting and repenting of the sin under Bunyan's view, or joining in humility and praise with a posture of rejoicing worship at a gospel truth.

MER: Exactly. Maybe a couple of contrasting examples would help round out this overview of the Pilgrimverse. Morden and Broomhall produce my favorite little devotional of forty reflections through Part I. It's user-friendly in providing short reflections, and it also shows it recent vintage by being the only devotional to peg Bunyan's text to John 3:16!

RES: Wow, that it interesting! So neither Bunyan nor his later preaching commentators had that proof verse as their first recourse in encouraging the gospel to Jesus followers. It goes to show, doesn't it?

MER: What does it go to show?

RES: Oh, sorry, well, it goes to show that one historical moment's key Bible verse is not necessarily another's, even though the fullness of the Bible and a common mission to proclaim good news unites those times.

CNA: Nicely said. And then, by contrast of size, Carolyn Staley's doorstopper of a 659-page commentary, *From Grace to Glory*, can represent the other end of the contemporary commentary spectrum.

MER: Staley gives sincere and gentle expression to the compassion of the Pastor's wife and Sunday School teacher. She reconfigures Bunyan's settings to modern scenarios to engage her readers while drawing out spiritual lessons.

CNA: So, she is very clear, early on, that Christian hasn't actually geographically abandoned his family. Rather he is transformed by the gospel and so apart from them spiritually.

MER: And we see glimpses of her present American setting when she imagines for her reader that the City of Destruction and the Town of Carnal Policy are all part of one urban complex, divided by a river, representing man's fallen state.

CNA: Despite this spiritualization, the details Staley lands on to describe Carnal Policy as the monument to "Human Reason" are intriguing: this is the city of fancy upmarket neighborhoods, museums and performance venues, elite universities and colleges, a colossal library, and a liberal judicial system. This is the town of humanistic philosophy.

MER: Combine those details with the horror of Staley's description of the City of Destruction's downtown, run to rack and ruin, where "if you drive through these sections of town by day you will notice" dereliction and security measures that tell you to avoid the place at night. What you get is an unspoken assumption that *Pilgrim's Progress* could not be for the kinds of people who didn't need to drive through downtown as tourists just because that was where they live.

CNA: Yes, the goods of spiritual life in Christ is subtly allied to a small-town vision of conservative life where cities are just bad, and from where Christians will rise up and flee, as witnessed in the suburbanization of middle-class evangelical Christianity in the US that creates idylls of semi-rural repose in economic proximity to jobs, but unpolluted by the challenges of systemic social strife.

MER: Preach, sister!

CNA: Looks like I am!

MER: And if we can, let's mention a set of devotional books that occupy very different ground than Staley's even as they emerge in the same country. They represent the fluent best of an irenic and ecumenical catholic evangelicalism.

CNA: You mean Curtis Freeman's *Pilgrim Letters* and *Pilgrim Journey*. Yes, so good. These are written by a professional theologian in the form of letters from the Interpreter to a young Christian preparing for believer's baptism and for further instruction into the mysteries of the faith.

MER: Just the very construction of the books as small hardbacks with dustcovers featuring William Blake's illustrations for *The Pilgrim's Progress* puts these in a different kind of category.

CNA: Each letter takes its departure from an image by William Blake, a passage from Bunyan's classic, and then exegetes Scripture and the historical tradition of Christianity writ large. Rather than sequential commentary on *The Pilgrim's Progress*, Freeman allows Bunyan's work to supply commentary on contemporary questions of discipleship, proving its on-going value in drawing readers to the Scriptures which must ultimately nourish pastoral theology.

MER: These are all very different approaches, but they do attest to the continued life of the original book in the church's mission and worship.

RES: That was a rousing report, if I may say so?

NAR: Yes, thank you, both. We do need to be wrapping this report up. And I want to just note a recent disappearance that deprives the present Pilgrimverse. Barry Horner has had a faithful ministry in the US and Australia commending Bunyan and particularly *The Pilgrim's Progress*. His outline study guide and revised and accurate text are available for purchase, but his more thorough commentary document that used to housed online is no longer accessible.

RES: Thanks, Narrator. Horner's pastoral angle suggested, in his writings, that academic study often missed Bunyan's theological point. Maybe that was a harsh judgment at times, but also an apt way of pointing out that academic research can focus on small details of history and social setting and even theological niceties, while the big issue of the spiritual import of Bunyan's message ends up underemphasized.

NAR: That brings us nicely around to Proverbs 15:30. The Pilgrimverse can strain to moral hectoring or strident preaching at times, and the mode of expression of Bunyan and his fans can age poorly when looked at centuries later. Yet, there is also a cheerfulness that emerges in the many ways that missionaries and pastors have sought to be agents of good news in bringing *The Pilgrim's Progress* into their ministries. The testimonies to the ways God, ultimately, uses Bunyan's work and its adaptations to reach and encourage are many.

RES: I can't help but bring us back to the Eva Hulbert's Probationer's Companion. Here are the Reverend Peck's summary comments on Vanity

Fair: "Wine, beer, amusements–nets. Go wrong because fail to consult the Bible." The unwary, he is saying, will be snared by the world's vices if they go wrong by failing to read and live out their Bibles. It's clear that whether evangelizing, commentating, meditating, or producing study guides, the Pilgrimverse has loads of fans whose primary draw to Bunyan's book is its biblical standing. And their primary goal in adding to the Pilgrimverse is to point to Scripture's truth for their audience.

NAR: Nice way to sum up the chapter, Researcher.

RES: Thanks, but I do have one last question for Christiana? I couldn't help but notice that your confidence, although befitting your claim in Part II to be a "risen Mother in Israel," after the judge Deborah, is still stronger than some would picture?

MER: Even I've noticed that! So, what gives?

CNA: That's a fair observation, guys. I'll come clean. I'm Christiana as portrayed in Kenneth Wright and Wayne Scott's Southern California LifeHouse Theater musical productions. I'm bolshie and stand for no nonsense. I quite like this me. Maybe we'll see more performances from the Pilgrimverse in a later expedition?

RES: I think that would be good.

NAR: I know it will happen, but not now. We're done.

Pilgrimverse Resources:

Barnard, Joe. *The Way Forward. A Road Map of Spiritual Growth for Men in the 21st Century*. Fearn, UK: Christian Focus, 2019.
Breakn Truth Ministries. "Pilgrims Progress: A Breakdancers Journey to Liberation," Apr. 24, 2018. https://www.youtube.com/watch?v=8sRfOEVdE8k.
Fernandez, Robert, dir. *The Pilgrim's Progress*. Revelation Media, 2019.
Ford, Cheryl. *The Pilgrim's Progress Discipleship Course*. Bloomington, IN: WestBow, 2016.
Freeman, Curtis. *Pilgrim Journey. Instruction in the Mystery of the Gospel*. Minneapolis, MN: Fortress, 2023.
____. *Pilgrim Letters: Instruction in The Basic Teaching of Christ*. Minneapolis: Fortress, 2021.
John, J. Pilgrim. *John Bunyan's The Pilgrim's Progress. A Contemporary Retelling*. Chorleywood: Philo Trust, 2012.
Morden, Peter, and Ruth Broomhall. *To Be a Pilgrim: 40 Days with "The Pilgrim's Progress."* Farnham, UK: CWR, 2016.
Staley, Carolyn. *From Grace to Glory: A Present Day Journey Through John Bunyan's "Pilgrim's Progress."* Port St. Lucie, FL: Solid Ground, 2019.

Further Reading with Mr Researcher:

Draycott, Andy. "Evangelical Devotionals and Bible Studies of *The Pilgrim's Progress* Fidelity or Bibliolatry?" *Christian Education Journal* 17:2 (Aug. 2020) 264–82.

Draycott, Andy. "Pilgrim's Missionary Progress: Contemporary Evangelistic Adaptations of John Bunyan's Lingering Spiritual Classic for a Post-Secular West." *Missiology* 49:2 (2021) 149–62.

Draycott, Andy. "Missional Pilgrim's Progress in Memory of Her: Representing Women in Adaptations of a Classic." *Evangelical Missiological Society Occasional Bulletin* (Spring 2020).

5

Home

My dear children, for whom I am again in the pains of childbirth until Christ is formed in you, how I wish I could be with you now and change my tone, because I am perplexed about you!

GALATIANS 4:19–20

I saw in my dream that Researcher was sat at his desk looking around expectantly, as if someone would pop up out of nowhere, which, in fairness to him, by now he had come to expect in his aided exploration of the Pilgrimverse.

RES: Who's around for the next bit of exploration, I wonder? Hello? Hello? Anyone about?

"We're here!" comes the cry from a young couple pulling themselves down from a pile of books and boxes.

RES: I'm not sure I recognize you, I'm sorry. I thought I knew the books well.

James: I'm James. And this is my wife Phebe. In fairness, Mr Researcher— Yes, we've heard about you—there's not a lot in *The Pilgrim's Progress* to identify us. Phebe is Gaius's daughter, and we are married at the end of our group's visit to his inn, along with my older brother, Matthew and Mercy. You know, in Part II?

PHEBE: We have been living in Beulah Land, near this side of the River of Death, since our traveling group came to the end of Part II.

JAM: Our kids are playing with their cousins at Matthew and Mercy's. She said she's had a really enjoyable Pilgrimverse adventure, so recommended we offer our services.

PHE: Yeah, we're hoping for a bit of fun, to be honest. The young parent of little kids gig feels pretty heavy on the responsibility front.

JAM: Mind you, because we are responsible, it would do us no harm to scope out ways in which the Pilgrimverse might hold out material that is formational and character-building.

RES: So fun and formational, you say? OK, we've been learning quite a lot about the Pilgrimverse, but haven't really focused in on family matters so far. Why don't you two have a look around and let me know what you find. Although, I must say, I feel it's a shame your kids aren't with you. You can probably find plenty of kid-oriented material in the Pilgrimverse.

PHE: Oh, we don't mind using a bit of couple time to check things out together. In fact, we will be a lot better off surveying things while the kids are occupied. We can give our parental assessment of any kid products we come across. Stress-free!

RES: All right, well, I appreciate the help. You can enter through a range of portals. I think that red covered kid's book might be a way in.

James and Phebe together walk over to a large book which they push open. To their surprise a dragon leers out at them. It turns out the book is a pop-up book called *Go with Christian!* and, mercifully, this is merely a cardboard image rather than Apollyon himself. Recovering from the shock, they take each other's hand, and laughing a little too hard in compensation, leap under the dragon's claws into the Pilgrimverse.

Researcher busies himself with a little desk tidying until, some while later, the pop-up book quivers before spewing out the cheerful couple again.

JAM: We've had a lot of fun!

PHE: But not just fun!

JAM: Some of the journey has also been instructive! And some a little strange, but we wandered far and wide. We reckoned the oldies probably hadn't covered as much territory so wanted to represent the younger generation well.

RES: That's great. I'm ready for your report.

PHE: Let's tell him about the pop-up book, *Go with Christian!*

JAM: Yes.

NAR: Sorry, guys, you'll just have to skip ahead—I've scheduled conversation about that book in the Pilgrimverse Sights expedition.

PHE: Oh, man! But it was so fun - we're definitely reading it to our kids, aren't we?

JAM: Absolutely. Okay, so you want us to be a little more serious. So how about this: first, we should tell you that we grew as a couple in this journey.

PHE: Yes, we didn't start off that well, we were so giddy at being without the kids that we both wanted to do our own thing.

JAM: We bickered about the direction we should go, and even what to spend more or less time exploring.

PHE: But, as I say, we grew, and, in part, this was in talking things out after both reading Annie Wald's *Walk With Me*.

RES: What's "Walk With Me," then?

JAM: Before we tell you about the book, we should remember a few details of the story of *The Pilgrim's Progress* that make it a pretty unlikely book.

PHE: Right, so remember that the stimulus for Christian's journey is not only the pull effect of conviction of sin in reading Scripture and heeding Evangelist's invitation?

RES: Yes.

PHE: It's also his dejection at being mocked and rejected by his wife and kids and neighbors who don't see any danger in continued living in the City of Destruction.

RES: Uh huh.

JAM: So, famously, the book starts with Christian leaving home and abandoning his family.

PHE: And, just another reminder that even those details of the family's response to his burdened complaints, and later accounts of his missing them, are additions that Bunyan includes only in the 2nd edition.

JAM: Which, in fairness, are changes he brings out fairly quickly, within a year of the first edition.

RES: Noted.

PHE: That alone suggests that spousal abandonment, even in an allegory where that dereliction is a metaphor of spiritual division brought about by the gospel, was probably not received without some criticism by Bunyan's first readers.

JAM: And some critics think Part II, our Part, while it might be driven by Bunyan's disgust at others faking their own sequels, is also an attempt at redemption on this score by an author who is deeply in love with his own wife and family.

PHE: Yes, our Part II is a companionable journey of our Mother, Christiana, her friend, now our sister, Mercy, and us kids, as well as a whole bunch of waifs and strays, as it were.

JAM: And, we get married, along with my older brother Matthew and Mercy, and then later, at Mnason's house, my younger brothers Samuel and Joseph get married to Mnason's daughters Grace and Martha respectively.

PHE: Let's just skip over the fact that that is a curious conjuring of time for Bunyan's plot. One minute these little boys are prone to naughtiness in stealing from a fruit tree, for example, and need escorting to their bed before the adults at night, and then the next they are of marriageable age.

RES: But, to be fair, Bunyan is not so worried about narrative coherence on the realist model of a novel. He is, however, interested in recognizing the goods of everyday discipleship. These include the good of marriage as a divinely ordained and companionable institution. In his Part II story, marriage is situated within the life of the church community, but still earns its spot as a key marker in the spiritual journey.

JAM: Anyway, this was all background to us telling you about a more recently written allegory that we found helpful too.

PHE: Annie Wald, trained professional counsellor, wrote an allegory of a journey made by a couple, Peter and Celeste. She calls it *Walk With Me* and it is subtitled "Pilgrim's Progress for Married Couples."

RES: Ok, we're back here, again. Tell me more.

JAM: On the back cover, Eugene Peterson blurbed the book saying, "parents preparing their children for marriage, pastors preparing their parishioners for marriage, and married couples who need a 'story' for their marriage will find this book a treasure."

PHE: And although we're not exactly newly-weds, we are young, and had kids pretty quickly, you know, in the seventeenth-century manner, so we still benefitted from Wald's advice.

RES: What kinds of things does it cover?

PHE: A big one was how to navigate the temptation to selfishness within a marriage. That is, how to avoid Selfishness Swamp.

JAM: And then avoid mutual recrimination in Revenge Chasm.

PHE: Ooh, yeah. We've been there, haven't we? Also, how to think about reconfigured relationships with parents. Which is relevant for me, even though James's parents have both passed through the River of Death.

JAM: I still have to deal with the in-laws!

PHE: Good point. It has practical advice about how to and how not to think about the biblical teaching on headship, and more importantly emphasizes that love is a choice within marriage and not just a feeling. The male pilgrim, Peter, on his wedding night, is counselled by a character called Discernment, "It's important to choose your partner wisely, but even more important to choose to love her every day."

JAM: And even if choice can make the marriage relationship sound a little too contractual, it's not a bad way of framing covenantal obedience as a daily calling.

RES: Do you know, this is coming back to me now. And you've reminded me that I was once reading Annie Wald's book in a line at a theme park and a man walked past the line and called out to me that the book was the best thing he'd ever read for his marriage. I regret now not being more like Christian and ditching my kids to run after him to find out more!

PHE: Well, I think we've given you the gist of the book. It's quite well done, and is a clear nod to Bunyan. Some of the metaphors are obvious, there's no honeymoon, but there is a "moon of honey"!

JAM: And, in case you are wondering, yes, Wald does address sex, but it takes a little while to work out that that is what the "chalice of delight," that the couple both drink from, is meant to represent.

PHE: Well, since you brought up sex, let's do the responsible thing and make the Pilgrimverse connection to family.

JAM: Fair enough, you romantic, you!

PHE: So, a little more tucked away, but perhaps even more thematically surprising is the Pilgrim's Progress parenting book.

RES: Again, let's go easy on Bunyan. To be fair, Part II does commend the home instruction in the faith that Christiana's boys, including you, James, have received that allows you to answer Charity's questions at the Palace Beautiful with good witness. That scene effectively showcases the kind of instruction in the faith known as "catechesis." Or you could picture it as an outline of a good Sunday School curriculum. This showcases Bunyan's commendation of the life of the church for nurturing a godly family.

JAM: Oh, for sure. We're definitely not going to knock Mom's single parenting skills.

PHE: But there actually is a book devoted to parenting that is built out of reflections on *The Pilgrim's Progress*. It's published in association with the conservative evangelical ministry set up by Dr James Dobson, Focus on the Family.

JAM: While Wald is pretty creative in her appropriation of Bunyan for a marriage allegory, Craig and Janet Parshall want to commend the gospel in parenting and, then, they also like Bunyan's classic. The idea seems to be that Bunyan gives lots of good gospel truths that Christian parents will want their children to know and believe. They use episodes from *The Pilgrim's Progress* to address the role of parents in guiding their children spiritually, steering them from temptation to pursue worthless things, warning about the possibility of persecution in a hostile culture because of their faith.

PHE: For example, the book opens with a chapter encouraging parents to pursue their children's understanding of the gospel of grace in Jesus Christ from the Bible, impressing on them, as appropriate, the need to make their own decision to "invite Jesus" into their heart. Faithful's run in with Wanton is the textual basis to discuss how to raise kids to understand their sexuality within a biblical morality; the battle with Apollyon occasions reflection on the Christian life as spiritual battle. Grace is brought up at the book's close so that a parental modeling of God's grace enables their kids to explain the gospel to unbelievers. All in all, although dated now, the book contains practical wisdom and action steps and resources to help Christian parents not tackle their child-raising alone or as a purely educational or physical developmental task.

PHE: Sometimes the welding of the book and parenting together is a little clunky, we must admit. But it's certainly true that Bunyan had a deep love of family and was not shy of recommending good practices, like in a book he wrote called *Christian Behavior*. Filled with sound advice, it is still shocking how outdated practical examples are from a book published in 2003 before the advent of the smartphone and data streaming.

JAM: That's a fair observation, although not a criticism of the book as such. Look, now we've mentioned marriage and parenting in the Pilgrimverse we should recognize the educational tentacles of home life. And that's because *The Pilgrim's Progress* is massively popular in the literature taught in the Christian homeschool networks of North America.

PHE: But this is, itself, a narrowing of its educational role from the late nineteenth and earlier twentieth century.

JAM: Good point. The book is amply evidenced as a text-book for middle or high schoolers when English curricula are getting off the ground for literary instruction. Often these books have comprehension questions at the back, or the annotations deal chiefly with Bunyan's upsettingly poor grammar and spelling!

PHE: It seems that the further that seventeenth-century English is removed from how we speak and write, the higher up the educational ladder the book moves. It is produced today with critical apparatus alongside other undergraduate textbooks, suggesting that it is now most profitably studied in courses such as Early Modern Literature or Transatlantic Puritan Culture.

PHE: Which is funny given how strongly it remains part of a push among Christian educators for younger children.

JAM: Although this will often be via adaptations.

PHE: But before turning to kids' adaptations for their owns sake, let's note, two contrasting examples of Pilgrimverse presentation to school kids that show the range of its applicability. Ruth Broomhall, in the UK, produced a curriculum booklet of seventy-nine pages, pitching *The Pilgrim's Progress* to ages five to ten years old in British primary schools. Although only some of these schools are church administered there remains a component of the curriculum given over to Religious Education which incorporates Christianity among other main religions. Broomhall's resource sets out differentiated, age-appropriate lesson plans.

JAM: She also provides a colorful wall chart of Bunyan's timeline. While this is a religion focused resource, the idea is that social studies, history as well as literature can be covered by a study of the book. It has a curricular richness, one might say.

PHE: She bases her outline of the plot on Jean Watson's *The Family Pilgrim's Progress* which is an adaptation to simplify language and theological discourse from the original.

JAM: So let's recognize that she is preparing a curriculum for use by teachers and students who may not be very familiar with Christianity or Bunyan.

PHE: Right, which is very different from the intended users of the Answers in Genesis homeschool curriculum from the US. At a colossal 492 pages the curriculum has multiple comprehension and interpretation work sheet questions paired with divided up sections of Bunyan's original text.

JAM: This resource, as it is laid out, is less interested in the historical aspect, and much more directly invested in the exhortation to Christian faith and living of a school setting that is closer to Sunday School than public school. Correspondingly, the discussion questions are more obviously leading, and more closely pegged to the Bible, than in Broomhall's product.

PHE: But, at the same time, being a homeschool curriculum, the notes to Instructors at the beginning of the book chart a comprehensive course on science and its early modern development, along with recommendations of history textbooks, and other language arts texts that would put this resource alongside a class in Mathematics as a full semester's work.

RES: Wow, those are both very impressive.

JAM: All this talk of instruction and teaching can make the Pilgrimverse home sound a little dull, but there are determined efforts among creative minds to keep *The Pilgrim's Progress* alive for homes in the guise of family fun.

RES: How so?

JAM: Well, mainly through games and play.

PHE: Before we get to the games, can I just mention the table top theater designs. These give kids and their older family companions the chance to enact the story using the assorted characters and backdrops. It's not too different from the old flannelgraph collection of felt characters designed for Sunday School use.

JAM: What is with you and school? We're supposed to be doing play right now!

PHE: Sorry, Ok, so let's report on the board games.

RES: Can I just say that I briefly saw that flannelgraph set on an online auction but couldn't afford to bid at the time? I'm still gutted it's not in my collection.

PHE: Well, you seem to have compensated pretty healthily by the collection on this desk!

RES: That's a fair call. Back to the board games.

    Seemingly out of nowhere, two characters appear and approach James and Phebe.

Mr Worldly-Wiseman: Is that our cue?

JAM: Yes. Great timing.

PHE: So, Mr Researcher, Sir, board games aren't so much fun for two people, so we recruited a couple of fellow players?

JAM: Let me introduce Mr Worldly-Wiseman and Pliable.

RES: It's a pleasure to meet you both. How many of these board games did you play.

JAM: There are two board games from the nineteenth century that we couldn't lay our hands on, so we stuck to games from the last one hundred years.

RES: That's still a decent spread.

W-W: And can I just register that some of us were more flexible with the rules than others.

RES: You didn't win, did you?

W-W: Not once! But then, my friend, Mr Legality, did teach me to be a stickler for the rules. In one game I just couldn't throw the right number on the die to ever get out of Doubting Castle, and I've never been given to self-doubt!

JAM: And Pliable won every game!

Pliable: What?! You've just got to know how to go with the game…

PHE: And cheat a little?

PLI: Look, I'm one of the biggest losers of the book, so you guys should give me a break!

RES: All right, guys. Tell me about these games.

W-W: They vary in complexity, but all have the general outline of a journey around the board from the City of Destruction to the Celestial City.

PLI: There are fun little ways that they manage to signal key moments in each player's progress. For example, at first I thought a game from the 1950s had a spinner instead of dice out of a fundamentalist fear of instruments of gambling, but then I realized it was a cleverer ploy. The spinner pointed to two levels of scores. Until the player had reached the cross, the inner ring of low scores had the progress limited to no more than 3 spaces at a time. The outer ring of scores kicked in once the burden was, as it were, lost at the cross, and now progress could speed up to 6 spaces at a time.

W-W: Another had the player piece change from a burdened image to a vigorous, sword carrying image. A simpler version of the same was having figurines whose plastic burdens are detachable.

PHE: Where the game route was more open to choice, it was still necessary to make sure to acquire a sealed scroll before eventually getting to the River before the Celestial City.

PLI: One game had River of Death cards which allow you to either ford the river or face capsizing from Captain Vain-Hope's boat. If you did you were "swept away over the falls to perilous pool," which was an earlier place on the board.

W-W: Not quite hell, but it's hellish to get on the shoot or snake, or whatever, when you're so close to winning.

JAM: Some games had supplemental guidebooks explaining the spiritual allegory of each of the locations on the board.

PLI: But you could play without paying too much attention to those. I guess that would be the province of an overbearing parent in a family game?

PHE: It's true that some of the spiritual hopes suggested in printing Bible verses on the board would only bear fruit if consulted independently of the simple game play. One version James and I particularly enjoyed incorporated the accumulation of cards representing Faith and Prayer and other spiritual disciplines. These, then, allowed you, if in your possession, to escape the consequences of the bad space landing.

JAM: In keeping with Bunyan's narrative, the challenges and threats to players through the Valley of the Shadow of Death got tougher as it progressed while Prayer was the most effective counter in that section of the board.

W-W: We were a little more ambivalent about the most intense role-player game board from Shepherd Solid Ground Games. What I loved about it was the crowding of the board with numbers and the thick spiral bound games-master guide book.

PLI: Unfortunately, the whole color scheme of the board and game book was overwhelmingly black, reproducing spookily emmeshed Victorian illustrations of *The Pilgrim's Progress*.

JAM: The Celestial City in the middle of the board had a shade of gold relief, and there was also a nice touch where the player pieces that were folded bits of card were turned inside out at the cross. Black and white Graceless became a gold haloed Christian, and Faithless, Faithful, and so on.

PHE: Yes, that was a well thought out touch. The two hundred-page spiral bound "play-action book" was the most intensely Scriptural for players. Each play location on the board had a page with a brief excerpt from the book, with an overall Bible verse, and then each possible throw of the die also came with an individualized Bible verse as well as instructions for proceeding in the game.

JAM: The schema for each turn of play is fascinating: the die throw points players to a chart of "providential results." The throw determines the outcome of the heart conflict between the "fruit of the spirit" and "works of the flesh" for that particular part of the turn. Following along the line corresponding numerically to the throw, the player reads from the "The Lord speaks" column and then complies with the action instructions from the "SO, RUN!" column.

PHE: And the turn only ends once the player reads aloud the scripture at the bottom of the page.

W-W: For me, it was just too wordy a distraction from the actual fun of playing a game.

JAM: But you are, to be fair, well known as an opponent of the Word, the Bible. So, despite the visual design faults, I think this could actually be a way of playing *The Pilgrim's Progress* that would appeal to Scripture-hungry Bunyan devotees.

PHE: But Mr W-W is right, don't you think, that it would not be a winner for multi-aged family games unless all were equally as committed?

JAM: I suppose so.

W-W: Thanks, Phebe.

RES: So what do you guys think, overall, are the goods served by these board games?

PLI: Winning is always fun!

PHE: Thanks, Mr Maturity!

JAM: I think Pliable has a point. Each game was winnable in about 45 minutes which means they fit well into a family or friend dynamic without being overlong.

W-W: Although I admit I show up on the boards as an obstacle in all these games, the point I'd make is that they all try different ways to represent the struggles and challenges of the Christian journey.

JAM: And to a lesser or greater degree they can gamefy the spiritual lessons that Bunyan allegorizes.

PLI: Which makes you realize that in some senses, the allegory is already a game. The ending is set out on the title page, but the journey is what provides the narrative interest, and the same is true of the board games.

RES: None of you mentioned the Pilgrim's Progress Bible Game by Doug Huffman?

JAM: Well, that's 'cos it has only the most dubious footing in the Pilgrimverse.

RES: How so?

W-W: It's just a board with a journey mapped as if it's about Pilgrim's Progress, but then the game has nothing to do with Bunyan's book.

JAM: Again, Mr W-W is a little sore about this one. Suffice it to say that it didn't scratch an itch of his.

W-W: Except in a bad way: it was a pure and simple Bible trivia game masquerading as a *Pilgrim's Progress* game! So annoying!

PHE: Which we actually thought wasn't too far from the way Bunyan does in fact throw into his narrative the randomest Bible verses and allusions.

RES: Well, thanks, guys. I can see that some of these must be fun. Anything else on the game front?

PLI: There's the computer video game, by Scott Cawthorn, who is more famous for being the creator of the *Five Nights at Freddy's* which has recently spawned a movie.

RES: OK, so who played this one?

PLI: That's all me. So, here's what I've got: we know this game is more geared to teens and adults by watching the playthrough videos on YouTube made by adult players. What's fun about the computer game is that there is ample deviation from Bunyan's narrative.

RES: So, it avoids the restrictions of a prior narrative that might make progress in the game boring, do you mean?

PLI: Yes. The game still starts in the City of Destruction, but here the player discovers one of several tasks to fulfil, and has to decide how to resource the pilgrim avatar by collecting points or prizes, and then how to equip him to survive combat with baddies. Different levels of play affect the way in which strategy between choosing to be equipped with prayer or faith and so on will determine one's success. What's fun is that the tasks range from giving out Bibles, mimicking Christian's proclamation mode in Part I, to feeding orphans which picks up on Mercy's acts throughout Part II. The player still has to shed their burden to reach the end of the game and this comes, as per the book, at the cross. The player's pilgrim avatar on the screen can not only move left and right, and jump, but can also kneel in prayer, with a down cursor, which is what unlocks access to the cross, for example. This is where the player choice element takes a back seat. An encounter with Jesus ensues at the cross where the player avatar asks for forgiveness of sins and receiving it, his burden falls from his back. This brings a blissful transformation of the scene, a return to the main game platform and the ability to leap and jump unencumbered.

RES: So there is a level of required interaction with Bunyan's gospel narrative?

PLI: Right, the game can't progress unless the spiritual encounter and transformation is undertaken by the avatar. On the plus side, you can see that this immersion in spiritual encounter, even virtually, can evoke identification and praise in the devout player. The down side being the long-suffering eye roll of any player just trying to negotiate the game.

JAM: Which given the wide availability of alternative games probably means this is for a Christian audience only, right?

PLI: I would say so. Even if some of those Christian kids may be more so culturally than in their hearts—so still subject to the impact of a game's message as Bunyan might have hoped if he'd been able to imagine such a product!

RES: It seems that the games, in all their formats, are made to entertain but also to teach. Did you find more that fits that teaching mode in the Pilgrimverse?

PHE: But the Pilgrimverse is also fun. I think that's why its religious message ultimately warrants adaptation for kids. Bunyan's good news that he wants to encourage believers in his day to hold onto, after all, is not that complicated.

JAM: At the same time, there is always a danger that a children's adaptation will turn the good news of grace into a behavioral manual.

PHE: Let's look at a few examples of children's adaptations to assess how they work.

NAR: And I'll jump in to advise the reader of this report that because children's adaptations are also the most illustrated of adaptations, there is overlap from this expedition into the one to come.

JAM: Wow, he even knows the future!

PHE: I know. Spooky, isn't it? Well, thanks, Mr Narrator. I guess we'll just carry on and you'll make sure to fix things for the next expedition.

NAR: Yes. Don't mind me. Just go ahead.

PHE: Thanks. Where were we?

JAM: Children's adaptations.

PHE: Yes. These have to cover a whole range of kinds of consumption. Books may be designed for read aloud while a young child is entertained by bright pictures. Or the story may be re-written to make the vocabulary easier for early readers.

JAM: Often you will get abridgement of the longer conversations that dig into theological themes that will not hold attention as much as the sequence of encounters and locations.

PHE: Some entertain their readers with rhyming couplets, which goes back to the congregationalist preacher, editor and illustrator George Burder in his 1803 Pilgrim's Progress versified, and is still going strong with Rousseaux Brasseur's "Poetic Adaptation" in 2020.

RES: Can you give us a flavor?

PHE: Sure, and see what you make of the register of language aimed at young readers in each:

Here's a little Burder on Christian and Hopeful's captivity in Doubting Castle:

> Well, thus the poor deserted prisoners lay
> All Wednesday, Thursday, Friday, Saturday.
> Resolv'd, at length, to pray; on God they call,
> And prostrate on the earth, before him fall.
> 'Twas midnight when they first began to pray,
> And on they wrestled, till the break of day.
> Then Christian starting up in glad suprize,
> "Why, what a monstrous fool I am !" he cries.
> "Here in this horrid dungeon to remain,
> "When in a moment I might freedom gain!
> "Here, in my bosom, lies a curious key–
> "'Twill open any lock–come, let us see."

And now a taster of Rousseaux Brasseur, a couple of centuries later, on the same episode:

> *Hopeful*: "My brother, that song and prayer have restored my soul;
> My heart is full of hope, and my joy is now full!"
> *Christian*: "Same for me! I feel free and refreshed and relieved.
> I remember all God's promises can be believed!"
> As he said that, he pressed his hand to his chest–
> And was blessed with the answer to their prayers and requests!
> *Christian*: "With my mind all cleared up, I've suddenly remembered
> A gift I was given at the place I was delivered!

> I was given this key, called the 'Key of Promise,'
> And was told it would free me from doubting like Thomas.
> We've been locked here in Doubting Castle for days,
> Yet around my neck, I had the key always!"

JAM: We might just note the obvious by saying that the Pilgrimverse has always had arresting poems at key points because Bunyan himself writes poems to scatter across both Parts I and II.

PHE: And then, even more invitingly for young eyes, the earliest illustrations, which as woodcuts occupied an entire page of the book, were also given short, little four-line poems that sit below them.

JAM: They kind of function as action and plot summaries at the visually and therefore narratively most arresting passages—the very ones to which child readers with a sense of adventure will be drawn.

PHE: We don't know for sure it these were written by Bunyan or commissioned by Nathaniel Ponder from an anonymous poet.

JAM: Bunyan would have known of them and not actively disapproved, I reckon, for them to be carried in his book in his lifetime.

PHE: So the pictures and poems, although not necessarily intended for children, extend the reach of the Pilgrimverse to younger people just by being a material part of the book read more readily by their elders.

JAM: Yes, whether in a library of many books or few, those with pictures will stand out, especially if they feature armor and giants!

PHE: Maybe we should mention that it is pretty clear that twenty-first-century Pilgrimverse games are way more niche products than the late Victorian board games. Not only is family entertainment massively changed via radio, TV, through to social media and content streaming, but, if it hasn't been registered yet, we know that Bunyan's work is just less well known and popular than it has ever been in the general population, even in its homelands of English speaking Protestantism in the UK or US.

JAM: Is this where you want to mention the card games?

RES: More games?

PHE: Well, yes, if that's OK? Just because I think it makes the point that Pilgrimverse games will today be countercultural in very significant ways, much more so than in earlier eras of reception.

RES: Go for it.

PHE: All right, then. In late 1937 the card game manufacturer, Castell Bros Ltd are about to launch their very popular *Snow White* card game as a tie in with Disney's animated movie arriving in the UK. And to further cash in on their claim to the family entertainment market they quickly issue a few more games. One, *Speed*, will become a classic. The *Snow White* game will get a reissue in 1950s. But, it's another game we want to focus on.

JAM: Drum-roll, please?

PHE: Very funny! It's no surprise that a mass market *Progress* card game is issued in their Pepys Series. It comes in a fancy cushioned box, with both a rules booklet and a booklet proudly presenting a "résumé" of the story of *Pilgrim's Progress*.

JAM: I love the attention to the accents in résumé! Ooh la la!

PHE: The deck is divided into four suits or "signs" of Crown, Sun, Moon, and Star, and then numbered 1–13. The "P" Progress card functions as a Joker with a portrait of John Bunyan. Each card has an illustration of an episode from Part I, and the summary booklet gives text to many but not all of those cards. In doing so, it extracts from Bunyan's text with some abridgement but no rewriting.

JAM: Again, the illustrator gives us the key encounters and Christian's companions and foes like Apollyon and Giant Despair, but the theological wrangling with Hypocrisy, Atheist, the Flatterer or Ignorance are not depicted.

PHE: The summary is not afraid of the overt Christian confession of Jesus Christ and his salvation and the hope of heaven. It even shows the site of the By-Way to hell.

JAM: And while Faithful faces flames of persecution, he is also shown riding his chariot to heaven.

PHE: But there's no stark warning of hell at the end of the pack. The final cards are happy and golden with Celestial glory.

JAM: All of which is to say that, entertainment wise, it makes commercial sense for a game manufacturer in the open market to sell a Progress game and even include the edifying primer to the book, which is assumed to be well known.

PHE: While, at the same time, elements of the presentation elide the final stark thrust of Bunyan's gospel warning to the ignorant.

JAM: Oh, and the game with the cards itself, has nothing to do with Pilgrim's Progress. The rules gives the tradition game of 7s and rummy where the deck of cards functions just as it would if decorated with the regular standard suits and design.

PHE: Yeah, there's that, true.

RES: And you guys are saying that this is a relic, right?

JAM: Yes. But having said that, there's actually a very recent deck of cards celebrating *Pilgrim's Progress*.

PHE: It's beautiful. But not so much a mass market game. Rather it's more of a collector's item.

RES: How is it different from the *Progress* game.

JAM: Well, this deck comes as a regular deck of cards, no rules or story overview. Like the plush box of the Castell Bros, this item is very well crafted.

PHE: The box has an embossed glistening gold on black and grey-green color scheme. An armored knight is seen in front of wooden door, engraved on its highest point with the date 1678 and the label Wicket Gate. There is a gothic quality to the intricacy of the various panels of the divisions of the box design, as if linking panels of an ornate stained-glass window.

JAM: I really loved the detail of the closing flap on the top of the box. It is embossed with a quote from the Author's Apology, "Dark clouds bring waters when the bright bring none."

PHE: It's as if Peter Voth, the designer, is recognizing that his ornamentation may be more elaborate than the low church simplicity of Bunyan's vision, but that it promises fruitful witness to the Pilgrimverse, for all that.

JAM: Like the Castell Bros deck, Bunyan is again, here, the Joker card design. The number cards keep a patterned design on the reverse, shaded differently according to suit, but the details come in the Aces and the face cards.

PHE: The Ace cards show elaborate architecture of four Pilgrimverse locations, Vanity Fair, Doubting Castle, Delectable Mountains, and Celestial

City. Then the face cards are more elaborate still. With two faces in the opposing half figures from waist height on a face card, Voth houses two Pilgrimverse characters on each card, giving twelve pairs across the deck.

JAM: And I like how Voth respects the logic of the King, Queen, and Jack cards. He gives the King cards pairs of godly characters, like Faithful and Hopeful, Evangelist and Interpreter, and nicely, Christian and Graceless. The Jacks pair Apollyon with Giant Despair, or Formalist and Hypocrisy, Talkative and Ignorance, but the Queen cards pose more of a challenge.

PHE: Yeah, it does show up the disproportion of women in the original texts of the Pilgrimverse that Voth is drawing on. So along with Christiana, Discretion, Prudence, Mercy, Piety and Charity, we also get a Shining One as a feminized angel, and most interestingly, or desperately, a King's Trumpeter.

JAM: At least he didn't get instrumentally sexist and give us a King's Harpist!

PHE: Very funny. I'm not offended, by the way. Because it's also fair to say that male characters amply supply the Jack cards without even turning to Judge Hate-Good and the whole of his Jury and court witnesses, or Flatterer, Atheist, and Mr By-Ends, for example. There's no real danger of having to resort to depicting Wanton or Madam Bubble on the Jack cards.

JAM: Good point, well made. This deck of cards is nicely done, but it's also not that thrilling of a fun game, as I look at it.

PHE: Not every home aspect of the Pilgrimverse has to be exciting. And it doesn't all need pitching at the youngest family members. The cards invite commentary on the story behind them by those who know. And a solitary game of patience might be just the thing to escape the busyness of family bustle.

RES: Point taken; I know you want to explore the way the Pilgrimverse is fun for kids. And I agree it can be in terms of games and images, but the truth is that many kids are only going to come across the book in some kind of teaching setting, where the book is, in some shape or form, forced on them.

PHE: There's nothing like being forced to read something in school to kill enthusiasm!

JAM: We found school textbook versions of *The Pilgrim's Progress* that were in heavy production with the rise of English Literature as a subject in the later Victorian period and into the early twentieth century. Their editorial notes are full of comments on proper grammar (often corrections of Bunyan's poor grammar) and expanding the students' vocabularies with glossaries. The books often come with chapter-by-chapter comprehension questions.

PHE: Intriguingly, they assume that the biblical allusions and the theology are still accessible and in need of no explanation to navigate the text.

RES: But if we switch from school to Sunday School, you might end up with a brilliant teacher, like Tom Welsch.

JAM: Who's that?

RES: Mr Welsch teaches a Sunday School class to youngster of various ages at Trinity Baptist Church in Montville, New Jersey, every year. He has done so for over 30 years. He composed a series of what he calls "ditties" to help them learn the sequence of the narrative by memorization and recitation. Do you want to hear a few?

JAM: Yes, please.

RES (reading):

> 1. A dreamer dreamed upon his bed;
> "What shall I do?" a poor man said.
>
> 2. Evangelist asks, "Why stand and wait?
> "Follow that light to the Wicket gate."
>
> 3. His family cries out; but they cry out in vain;
> With fingers in ears, Pilgrim runs toward the plain.

RES: He has sixty-seven ditties in total that cover all of Part I.

PHE: Those are cool. Thanks for sharing.

RES: You're welcome. Look, I think it's time to wrap this up. I must say, you've said very little about the one area of the Pilgrimverse I thought would yield the most interest.

PHE and JAM: Oh?

RES: I mean children's books. Surely there are a ton of them?

NAR: That's my fault. I've arranged for those to be covered in the expedition exploring the visual elements of the Pilgrimverse sights. And there's also a decent amount written about them, too, unlike other areas of the Pilgrimverse, so I'll point to some resources in the write up of this report.

RES: OK, well, thanks, I guess. Any closing thoughts from my explorers?

JAM: Well, there is one more book I want to mention—although it's definitely on the margins of the Pilgrimverse.

RES: Go for it.

JAM: Family life is, on many accounts, a haven from the world and its demands. At the same time, the household is part of wider society and its economy. So, although it might seem strange, we're going to end our report with *The Business Pilgrim's Progress* by Colin Turner. The book's subtitle is "From a World of Mediocrity Towards the Land of Prosperity" with the byline, "How to give better-than-excellent service and receive greater-than-expected rewards."

PHE: This is not the book for those scholars who have identified the Vanity Fair episode as anti-capitalist tirade against markets and commodification.

JAM: Although it could lend support to those, on the other end of the spectrum, who claim Bunyan's business like language of "closing with Christ" is evidence of a nascent commodification of faith along capitalist lines.

RES: Wow!

PHE: I know. This is actually a fairly typical business self-help book but set up as an adaptation of *The Pilgrim's Progress*.

JAM: So Chris, obviously, sets off, as the subtitle says, "From a World of Mediocrity towards the Land of Prosperity."

PHE: But hold on. Don't omit the full title. It has very seventeenth-century vibes, because it goes on even further: "How to give better-then-excellent service and receive better-than-expected rewards."

JAM: Chris has to get from the town of "Apathy," up the Hill of Reluctance, across the "Valley of Embarrassment," to eventually reach Service City.

PHE: Each chapter has multiple call out gems of wisdom and ends with a set of bullet points informing the reader how "To Be a Pilgrim. . ."

JAM: Reaching the City of Service, it is no surprise to learn that the Customer is King, all customers are treated royally.

PHE: But the most jarring juxtaposition against Bunyan's text is that Chris arrives with his team of Spontaneity and Self-Reliance, each having realized their hidden potential to thrive for the customer's benefit and ready to receive the banker, Support's, investment.

JAM: 'Cos really, if anyone is Self-Reliant in *The Pilgrim's Progress* it is Ignorance. And we know the only reward he gets is Hell.

PHE: The trouble may not be so much with the Business wisdom deployed throughout the book, but the shoehorning of it into a story designed to do something very different—of an eternal rather than secular and temporal scope.

RES: Fancy words, Phebe. You're starting to sound like me!

PHE: That definitely means it's time to wrap this up.

JAM: It's been good to help us understand the managerial logic that can creep into the life of family and marriage when planning for success replaces faithfulness to the one whose future it all is. James warns, "Now listen, you who say, 'Today or tomorrow we will go to this or that city, spend a year there, carry on business and make money.' Why, you do not even know what will happen tomorrow."

RES: Now it is important to recognize that *The Pilgrim's Progress* has always been a market product, even in the notoriously unprofitable book business. It is not, then, unBunyanesque to buy, sell, and trade. Nevertheless, the proliferation of ephemeral products marketed to those with disposable income and or time (in the case of homeschooling) is a testament to the middle-class lives and aspirations of so many in the Pilgrimverse. Furthermore, it is not beside the point to invoke Vanity Fair of Part I as a critique of the idolatrous tendency to instill meaning in commodities that only the truth should bear.

NAR: So are we landing this chapter on a critical, negative note or a celebration of domestic life?

RES: Well, it can be argued that books and board games and even jigsaw puzzles are just devices to facilitate godly family conversation around the truth that is otherwise under threat with TV and phone streaming and social media.

NAR: OK.

RES: If we take our thoughts back to the opening passage from Galatians that you gave us, Mr Narrator, I'm struck that the Pilgrimverse home has both an affectionate and an improving tone. Paul calls the Galatian Christian "My dear children," and then comments on the struggle to see them formed in a Christlike way. Then he mentions his perplexity as an expression of frustration. This is what family life is like. In a similar way, Bunyan means his text to be encouraging and reproving. Be like this, know God is for you, and don't be like this because that way leads to destruction.

NAR: Do you see the products James and Phebe discovered contributing to that goal?

RES: Yes, in many ways. I will say that I have a hope that just as the Galatians would gain most from an in person encounter with Paul, so those who encounter *The Pilgrim's Progress* through board games or educational adaptations, curricula or even card games would finally benefit from engaging the full text in time.

NAR: But you don't think that is likely?

RES: I have my doubts. Lengthy classics that seem worthy but dull just by virtue of being classics will be off putting to many. Required texts in an adaptive form can have the effect of dooming the full thing to obscurity by being somewhat known. So maybe the Pilgrimverse's reach, out to youngsters and into family life, is hopeful in sharing some of Bunyan's dream with those who may not meet him elsewhere.

NAR: Well said. Let's let James and Phebe get back to relieve their babysitters. Thank you all.

Pilgrimverse Resources:

Brasseur, Rousseaux. *The Pilgrim's Progress. A Poetic Retelling of John Bunyan's Classic Tale*. Eugene, OR: Harvest House, 2020.

Broomhall, Ruth. *The Pilgrim's Progress: A Curriculum for Schools*. Bedford, UK: Palace Beautiful Ltd., 2016.

Bunyan, John. *Bunyan's Pilgrim's Progress Versified, With Explanatory Notes by George Burder*. 2nd ed. London and Edinburgh: T. Williams, and Button and Son, 1804.

Cawthorn, Scott. *The Pilgrim's Progress Video Game*. Hope Animation, 2011.

Dowley, Tim. *Pilgrim's Progress: The Game*. Board Game. Candle Books, 2008.

Fazekas, Steven, et al. *All-in-One Curriculum for The Pilgrim's Progress*. Petersburg, KY: Answers in Genesis, 2006.

Parshall, Craig, and Janet Parshall. *Traveling a Pilgrim's Path: Preparing Your Child to Navigate the Journey of Faith*. Wheaton, IL: Tyndale House, 2003.

Shepherd Solid Ground Games. *Race of Faith in the Similitude of a Dream*. 2005. Board Game.

Turner, Colin. *The Business Pilgrim's Progress*. London: Hodder, 2000.

Voth, Peter. *Pilgrim's Progress Playing Cards*. https://www.behance.net/petervoth/.

Welsch, Tom. *Pilgrim's Progress Ditties*. https://www.professorpilgrimsprogress.com/tom-welsch-s-ditties/.

Further Reading with Mr Researcher's friends:

Gulya, Jason J. "Teaching with *The Pilgrim's Progress* Video Game." In *Adapting the Eighteenth Century*, edited by Sharon R. Harrow and Kirsten T. Saxton, 95–108. Martlesham, UK: Boydell & Brewer, 2020.

Jackson, Gregory S. "A Game Theory of Evangelical Fiction." *Critical Inquiry* 39:3 (Mar. 1, 2013) 451–85.

Murray, Shannon. "Playing Pilgrims: Adapting Bunyan for Children." *Bunyan Studies* 18 (2014): 78–106.

6

Sounds

We have spoken freely to you,[...] and opened wide our hearts to you. [...] As a fair exchange—I speak as to my children—open wide your hearts also. Do not be yoked together with unbelievers. For what do righteousness and wickedness have in common? Or what fellowship can light have with darkness? What harmony is there between Christ and Belial?

2 Corinthians 6:11, 13–15

I saw in my dream that Faithful appeared at the corner of Researcher's desk, marching forward at a fair clip. Hopeful had lagged behind Faithful on their way down from the graphic novel adventure a while ago. He tried calling after him as Christian had done: "Ho, ho, So, ho! stay, and I will be your Companion.'" But Faithful just kept on walking as if he couldn't hear him. So Hopeful set to running and overtook his friend, and then started walking backwards in front of him so as to engage him in conversation. He managed quite a few agile steps like this, all the while speaking to, or at least at, Faithful, who appeared as if in a trance. And then, just as he thought to himself how much better than Christian he was at overtaking, Hopeful tripped up and fell clumsily on his back. It was only then that Faithful seemed to register his companion at all. He bent down while also removing something from his ears.

FAI: Are you ok?

HOP: What do you think? I'm lying awkwardly on the ground. . . . Yes, I'm fine. Give me a hand.

FAI (Helping Hopeful up): You remind me of Christian. I reckon the only thing hurting is your pride.

HOP: Thanks for that comparison. It came before the fall, right? Look, why didn't you listen to me when I called after you?

FAI: Oh, sorry about that. I was listening to Bryan Sibley's 2004 BBC radio dramatization. It's a noise-filled festival for the ears.

HOP: What were those things in your ears?

FAI: Just my earbuds. You should get some. They're noise-canceling.

HOP: Huh?

FAI: Oh, that just means that they cancel out any noise from outside so all you hear is the sound you're playing through the earbuds. Anyway, maybe I should take them out. When I stop to think about it, they might make the rest of our adventure a little antisocial. Bunyan would have had much less to write if Christian had just blocked out external chatter as he marched ahead.

I see that the two walk on together in silent thought, only broken after a while.

FAI: Now I think about it, the original traveling in our books was pretty quiet, wasn't it?

HOP: Now you come to mention it, I think you're right. It does seem like the only noise was mostly when we would speak.

FAI: That does make sense. Bunyan writes a lot in dialogue, but very little in the descriptive narration of sounds or the color of surroundings.

HOP: I mean, we do get some reference to "doleful noises," and there's a deal of crying out, but the soundscape of the narrative is not that developed.

FAI: Don't forget the "hubbub" at Vanity Fair!

HOP: I won't, I was there, you know. Anyway, are you suggesting that a dramatization supplies more feeling, if you know what I mean?

FAI: Absolutely. Let me give you an example from Sibley's drama. He very cleverly intersperses the story of the book with the story of Bunyan's arrest, trial and imprisonment. This gives opportunity for the sounds of creaking jail doors and clanking keys. It merges the fictitious, not unlikely,

Sounds

event of the prisoner's fever with the feverishly fearsome construction of Christian's battle with Apollyon. The soundscape of the battle is starkly harsh, with percussive bursts of discordant sound upon eerie lingering background strings, stomping feet, distorted monstrous voice for the beast, and querulous shouting Christian, fizzing fiery darts. The set up as a fever induced nightmare fits the original's dream setting while providing escalating drama to the encounter. The battle is overlaid with the angelic voice of Prudence from the Palace Beautiful advising Christian to put on the armor of God - the same voice actor is used for Prudence and one of the Angels in the casting. She provides a kind of internal coaching to the struggling pilgrim, just as the drama has Bunyan's wife, Elizabeth, visiting to tend to his fever in jail.

HOP: Wow, that's a lot of convey!

FAI: Yeah, it's really well done. But there aren't just the sounds of dramatic performance in the Pilgrimverse.

HOP: Oh? What else is there?

FAI: I can stream several different music albums devoted to *The Pilgrim's Progress*.

RES: And don't forget audiobooks, friends.

FAI: Hadn't seen you come in! Hi, Researcher. So what's the task today?

RES: Well, sound and music has the benefit of adding emotional tone or depth to mere narration. So we're exploring the stirring quality of sound in the Pilgrimverse, if you're up for it?

HOP: Maybe we should jump into this dimension with audiobooks, then, and expand our survey from there.

Looking around for a likely portal, the two explorer's spot Mr Researcher's open laptop, his browser open at a music streaming app. Without hesitation, these seasoned explorers just step into the screen and disappear into the Pilgrimverse. They are back almost as quickly. Evidently the Pilgrimverse is giving up its evidence at the speed of the fastest online downloads.

HOP: Mr Researcher, I hope you are ready, because our ears are drenched with the sounds of the Pilgrimverse. We said we'd start with audiobooks as they stay closest to the original book's format. So, what did we find, Faithful?

FAI: There are fairly loosely produced free audio books by LibriVox on platforms like YouTube, with solo narration or a dramatized version of multiple readers. Billed as an effort "to make all books in the public domain available, narrated by real people and distributed for free, in audio format on the internet," the quality does vary, shall we say.

HOP: But, if you stop to think about it, it's at the level of ordinary speech that the sound of the book first resonates. After all, from its early days it has been a book as often read aloud as read silently.

FAI: And this means that the voices of the narration and dialogue have changed as English and then other languages receive the book as an oral performance.

HOP: This is certainly true in terms of the audio recordings we've explored of the Pilgrimverse.

FAI: Yes, whenever Sir John Gielgud plays Christian, and he does a number of times in his career, a mellifluous Shakespearean theatricality affects the ears.

HOP: Fancy word! Mellif-what?

FAI: It means sweet and smooth.

HOP: You couldn't just have said that?

FAI: Ok, I'm sorry. Gielgud's tone and the musical accompaniment of Ralph Vaughan Williams's classical compositions place these recordings among the exhibits of a cultured elite.

HOP: Whereas, for example, when Peter and Anne Woodcock record an adapted retelling of Pilgrim's Progress for kids their voices are much more like the common voices of the everyday English speaker.

FAI: English English speaker, you mean!

HOP: Hmm?

FAI: Well, English is spoken by far more people than the English.

HOP: True. In fact, David Shaw Parker's audiobook of Part I, is a narration by one voice in many different voices, as it were. There's great versatility in voicing many different characters in this kind of recording. Shaw Parker portrays Faithful as Scottish, for example.

FAI: The Welsh get Evangelist in John Rhys-Davies's voice-over for the Robert Fernandez 2019 CGI movie.

Sounds

FAI: And in the same movie, Northern Ireland gets the Interpreter with the voice acting of singer Kristyn Getty.

HOP: And, of course, there are American narrations.

FAI: Max McLean gives his audio narration less of a variety of dialect and accent than Shaw Parker does. McLean's recording is described by the publisher as a "lively, heartfelt reading," but its relatively somber pacing and delivery misses some of the dramatic potential of Bunyan's characterizations.

HOP: You say that, but Bunyan himself, in fairness, makes little effort to alter the speech patterns in his text for different characters.

RES: Much as our dreaming narrator hasn't bothered with much differentiation of speech-patterns between us in this book, right?

FAI & HOP (together): Ummm. . . . If you say so . . .

RES: See?

FAI: And we need to recognize again that we are limiting our listening to English.

HOP: And it is always worth remembering that British or North American English does not account for the largest number of readers of English texts like Pilgrim's Progress. More fitting as a representative of that reality might be the Indian Christian vlogger, Arpana Saladi who has a narrating of part of Part I of *The Pilgrim's Progress* over twelve episodes on YouTube.

FAI: Fair point.

HOP: Can we just register that there is a difference between an audiobook narration and a dramatization. The latter takes creative liberties in presenting the story rather than the verbatim text.

FAI: Yeah, so John Pappas Jr.'s Californian recording using multiple actors is an "amplified version."

HOP: This kind of dramatization can give the action of the sound track greater "realism" but in this instance it is offset by the fake "ye olde" English which has awkwardly ungrammatical phrases like "my burden liketh to destroy me." Bunyan does use "like" in the way that today's English speakers would use the word "likely" at times, as in "is like to destroy me," but the punt to adding "eth" to the end of a verb to make it archaic is taxing on the ears, for little profit, in my opinion.

FAI: Here's a practical opinion for you: since you just fell over: listening to Pilgrimverse sounds in audiobooks means that pilgrims can make progress on the move without walking into obstacles while holding a book.

RES: Talking of being on the move, I've worked out that I could run the equivalent of a marathon from the City of Destruction to the Celestial City with David Shaw Parker at 1.5 times speed!

FAI: Have you?

RES: What?

FAI: Run a marathon listening to *The Pilgrim's Progress*?

RES: Well, no, but that's not the point. . . . I mostly listen to music when I run. So why don't we turn there?

HOP: We can certainly tell you a thing or two about hymns.

RES: All right, then. Tell me a little about that hymn singing.

FAI: So, from a twenty-first-century perspective, it could appear that *The Pilgrim's Progress* is a one-hit wonder, and even then that wonder is not without its problems.

RES: You means someone's taken Bunyan to court for plagiarizing his lyrics?

FAI: No, that's not what I mean.

RES: The music, then? Did he steal the melody from someone?

FAI: Hold on there. This is getting out of hand. There is an issue about the lyrics that I'll get to now, but Bunyan didn't write any music that we have record of. In fact, the hymn that is most often still sung of his didn't get used as a hymn until the 1860s, and it was set to its most popular tune in the early twentieth century.

HOP: That tune is called "Monk's Gate," by the way. And you'll hear it as the background melody to many audio performances of the book.

RES: So, to be clear, we're talking about "To be a Pilgrim," right?

FAI: Yes, although it's often known by its first line, which, when it became popular in hymn books, was "He who would valiant be."

HOP: But that wasn't how Bunyan wrote it in Part II, was it?

FAI: No. In fact, lots of more recent hymn collections have gone back to Bunyan's original phrasing, so the hymn then gets referred to as "Who would true valour see."

RES: What's the difference?

FAI: (Handing over a piece of paper) Well, I've printed out the two sets of lyrics side by side so you can see. Check this out:

Who would true Valor see,	He who would valiant be
Let him come hither;	'gainst all disaster,
One here will Constant be,	let him in constancy
Come Wind, come Weather.	follow the Master.
There's no Discouragement,	There's no discouragement
Shall make him once Relent,	shall make him once relent
His first avow'd Intent	his first avowed intent
To be a Pilgrim.	to be a pilgrim.
Who so beset him round,	Who so beset him round
With dismal Stories,	with dismal stories
Do but themselves confound;	do but themselves confound,
His strength the more is.	his strength the more is.
No Lion can him fright,	No foes shall stay his might,
He'll with a Giant Fight,	though he with giants fight;
But he will have a right,	he will make good his right
To be a Pilgrim	to be a pilgrim.
Hobgoblin, nor foul Fiend	Since, Lord, thou dost defend
Can daunt his Spirit;	us with thy Spirit,
He knows he at the end	we know we at the end
Shall Life Inherit.	shall life inherit.
Then Fancies fly away,	Then fancies fly away;
He'll not fear what men say;	I'll fear not what men say,
He'll labor Night and Day	I'll labor night and day
To be a pilgrim.	to be a pilgrim.

HOP: Those adapted lyrics, on the right, were by Victorian hymn-writer, Percy Dearmer, who decided that churches wouldn't be inclined to sing about Hobgoblins.

FAI: And you can see his theological intent is to be clearer about Jesus, or at least, the Master, and to invoke God as Lord and call upon the Spirit. That's way more Trinitarian than Bunyan's original.

HOP: True, but it does leave the singer wondering what "Fancies" might be, 'cos in the original that must be referring to the hobgoblins and foul fiends that have been erased from the sanitized version.

FAI: Well, we can report that nowadays when churchy people are, for example, gathering to record BBC Television's religious broadcast slot *Songs of Praise*, they are singing the original version of the words.

HOP: But when we find the hymn in fancier social settings, the less hobgoblinny, sanitized version prevails. That's true of Winston Churchill's state funeral and Margaret Thatcher's memorial service. It's also true of memorial service for the late crown consort, Prince Philip, Duke of Edinburgh.

FAI: And just in case your inclinations are not so politically conservative as Churchill and Thatcher or as establishment as Prince Philip, the hymn featured also in the funeral service of another former British Prime Minister, this time the left of center, Labour Party leader, Clement Attlee.

HOP: And that's not the end of the hymn thing in the Pilgrimverse.

FAI: Right! John Newton, you know, the former slave trader turned pastor, wrote "The Burdened Sinner," just around the time he resumed some lecturing on *The Pilgrim's Progress* to his Olney congregation in the winter of 1772. That was the week before he wrote "Amazing Grace."

HOP: Yeah, but despite its title, "The Burdened Sinner" at best only mildly alludes to Bunyan's text in its lyrics, most obviously when congregants are invited to sing, "Guilt makes me unable/ To stand or to flee."

FAI: That's probably why that hymn wasn't included in the edition of *The Pilgrim's Progress* for which Newton wrote a preface.

HOP: Good point. That edition did include a number of poems by Newton, and by his friend William Cowper, most of which are also then included as hymns in the collection of Olney Hymns that was important to Calvinistic evangelicals of the time.

FAI: One of Cowper's is called the "Shining Light" which riffs off of Evangelist pointing to the Wicket Gate and the "Pilgrim way" with these lines,

> When I review my ways,
> I dread impending doom;
> But sure, a friendly whisper says,
> "Flee from the wrath to come."
>
> I see, or think I see,
> A glimmering from afar;
> A beam of day that shines for me,
> To save me from despair.

And then there's the hymn called "The valley of the shadow of death" which starts,

> My soul is sad and much dismayed;
> See, Lord, what legions of my foes,
> With fierce Apollyon at their head,
> My heavenly pilgrimage oppose!

And then it goes on to address the spiritual torment of experiencing "fiery arrows" that shake the soul with "storms of blasphemies and lies."

HOP: Not very comforting for the congregations, I wouldn't have thought.

FAI: I hear you on that, but, on the other hand, it is also not as artificially and relentlessly upbeat as some contemporary sung worship experiences, either.

HOP: Ouch. Point taken.

FAI: And in this part of the Pilgrimverse hymns abound. Evangelicals were the main commentators on *The Pilgrim's Progress* in the nineteenth century and they were also hymn singers, so it's no surprise to see commentary on the book interspersed with snippets of hymns from stalwarts of the era like Isaac Watts, Charles Wesley, and even John Newton himself. And this carries on to today: Ken Puls is a contemporary musician who also has a devotion to *The Pilgrim's Progress*. He has built a whole website of commentary on the book, but for now we can note his original hymn lyrics.

HOP: The melody is simple as befits congregational singing. Each verse begins "Lord, we pray for those . . ." and then follows with a description of the situation of discipleship set out in most key episodes of Part I of *The Pilgrim's Progress*.

FAI: "A Prayer for Pilgrims" (©Ken Puls Music, 1993) has sixteen verses, much more in keeping with those hymns of Evangelical revivalists than today's shorter worship songs. Its recording on the website clocks in at over 10 minutes, but it has a gentle narrative quality to it so that the simplicity of the musical arrangement allows the repetition to focus the singer on the developing story told in the words. For example, the verse dedicated to the Doubting Castle episode goes:

> Lord, we pray for those imprisoned
> By Despair, who lie in grief;
> Locked in Doubting Castle's dungeon,

> Stripped of hope and its relief.
> Father help them to remember
> In Your promise is the key;
> Now unlock the door that bars them,
> In the Gospel, set them free.

You get the sense that a congregation patient in prayer would appreciate this structure and arrangement.

HOP: But maybe we should leave hymns behind now, to showcase the other musical forms that are out there?

FAI: On that note, if you'll pardon the pun, I think I might want to tag out of this search. To be honest, I enjoy the music, but I think we need someone more musical. Maybe we could switch out for Mercy?

HOP: She's a decent singer.

FAI: In fact, why don't we go find her. We'll send her over, Mr Researcher. She'll be up for it, I'm sure.

In my dream, Faithful and Hopeful disappeared among the Pilgrimverse artefacts, and Researcher waited for Mercy to appear. He is surprised when instead of the young woman he had seen just a few expeditions ago, he is approached by an older man, of very upright bearing. He recognized him from Part II. He was Mr Valiant-for-truth.

RES: I thought Mercy was coming. She's all for singing and dancing. She'd be great to explore this part of the Pilgrimverse.

Valiant-for-truth: What do you mean? She just told me that I should come out and find you, Mr. Researcher, because she was feeling really tired from some previous adventure you'd gotten her into. To be honest, I'm pretty sure I'm not your guy. You see . . .

They are interrupted by the sweet sound of singing, as a young chap carrying what must be described as a shepherd's crook wandered up to them. This was essentially a long walking stick like staff with a wide hook at the top end, all carved, it seemed, from one piece of wood. It had a worn look to it, immediately setting it apart from how you might imagine a ceremonial bishop's staff might look. As he approached he switched to whistling softly.

RES: Hello, Shepherd fella. What's your name?

Shepherd boy: Well, the best I can offer is Shepherd boy. I have a very small cameo role in Part II.

VFT: But at least you're a singer, 'cos as I was about to say . . .

SB: Thanks for noticing that. I do sing well, as it happens. In fact, my song . . .

VFT: The song John Bunyan wrote for you!

SB: That's right. My song has been sung as a hymn by thousands. You've probably been talking about it already?

RES (looks away awkwardly, muttering): Nope, just Valiant-for-truth's song, actually

VFT: Doesn't look like it, SB. You didn't realize that no one has heard of your song anymore?

SB: I think it would be fair to say that popular taste has overlooked my genius.

VFT: You're a one hit wonder, is what you're saying?

RES: Mr Valiant-for-truth, you seem a little on edge. Why so belligerent?

VFT: I'm sorry.

SB: And for your information, I get bumped up to Part I, by Edward Sackville-West's BBC Radio play for which no less than classical composer Ralph Vaughan Williams prepared the score. I serenade Christian to sleep at the leafy Arbor halfway up the hill Difficulty.

VFT (Still tetchy): Yeah, well, did you make it into his opera of *The Pilgrim's Progress* that premiered only a decade later?

SB: This isn't all about me, is it, Mr Researcher?

VFT: You didn't, did you? Make it into the opera, that is? My words do, you know, "To be a Pilgrim," and all that?

RES: OK, I think you might both work better in exploring the Pilgrimverse if you just stop the boasting and sniping.

SB: All right. I'm sorry.

VFT: Me too. It's just that this is all a horrible mistake. I know the words Bunyan gave me have been set as a hymn that has lasted. No offence, SB.

RES: I was actually just talking about "To be a Pilgrim" to Faithful and Hopeful.

VFT: Yes, that's the one. I'm not going to sing it. You can't make me!

RES: I wasn't going to. We've already . . .

VFT: You see, the thing is, I didn't actually sing those words. It was more of a devout poem-prayer or rhyming, rousing cheer for my fellow pilgrims. Now it is true that Bunyan likes a good sing-song. Specifically, he writes that others sing: Christian sings at the cross, Palace Beautiful is full of singing, there's a good bit of singing and dancing when Giant Despair is beheaded in Part II. Gosh, Mercy even breaks into song at the gallows, for pity's sake!

SB: And your point is?

VFT: I just don't have much of a singing voice, and certainly no musical skill or training.

RES: Don't worry about that, that doesn't disqualify you at all. There's every indication, like you say, that Bunyan loved music, and churches have sung his and your words over the centuries, but, think about it: that is bound to have included a ton of people who weren't great singers. In fact, it's probably more in keeping with Bunyan's congregational outlook of Christian discipleship than any great talented solo, no disrespect to Shepherd boy here.

VFT: Well, I guess that's true.

RES: So why don't you two bury the hatchet and see if you can't find out some fun things about the stirring world of musical performance in the Pilgrimverse. You just need to be aware of various media for accessing this area. There's a ton of recordings now to find on the internet as well as information about more intangible records of performances uncaptured by official recording. There are still CDs and DVDs out there too, and no doubt cassettes, VHS, and vinyl if you could find the technology to play them.

SB: So, do you have any guidelines about how we are to go about assessing what we hear?

RES: Well, there have a been a growing number of theological engagements with music in recent years but it is often at the elite level rather than the popular. And with no disrespect to Bach and Beethoven, I don't think it's controversial to suggest that Bunyan's book's feel is, at least originally, on the popular end of cultural expression. He owes his imagination more to ballads and cheap adventure "chapbooks" than to Shakespeare or Spencer, Herbert or Donne, or even Milton, for that matter.

VFT: OK, so we can think on the popular level?

RES: Exactly so, just try to give me a sense of the music's feel. Does it stir you in some way? I know that stirring is vague, but it could mean it makes you dance or sway or hum or, I don't know, cry, but in a good way.

SB: Or not!

RES: Well, possibly. But let's be charitable, 'cos Narrator's readers are going to have a range of musical tastes themselves, I don't doubt.

I saw in my dream that they were standing on the Researcher's desk just in front of a slightly worn looking CD-cassette-radio player, with a few CD cases and cassettes piled alongside it. Even though the Researcher's laptop was within reach on a stand, the two Pilgrimverse pilgrims couldn't help but be drawn to the bold color and design of the CD player. Valiant-for-truth boosted Shepherd boy up, who then pinged open the CD player lid by leaning heavily on its catch. Shepherd boy gained a purchase on the edge of the player to help Valiant-for-truth scale up, and then they both jumped into the machine, a portal to the performance world of the Pilgrimverse.

As ever, Researcher was left on his own to wonder what they would find.

Soon enough, the two pilgrim's re-emerged from the CD player ready to report.

SB: Ugh! I'm trying to shake off the ear worm effect of producers overdoing the "olde worlde" feel by pushing Christian's setting back a century for some Tudor "Greensleeves" vibes.

VFT: Yeah, there's only so much lute a person's ears can take!

RES: It might be a bit much to blame a Vaughan Williams tribute tendency on that move, right?

SB: Ooh, I like what you did there! Get it, Valiant-for-truth? 'Cos Vaughan Williams composes a *Fantasia on Greensleeves* as well as all those Pilgrim's Progress themes dotted throughout his symphonies.

VFT: Oh, stop showing off, will you!

SB: Sorry.

RES: Yes, sorry.

VFT: It's a different sound, but Maddy Prior's folk rendition of "Who would True Valor See" lifts the song away from stuffy, slow organ music to the bombastic potential the tune has—even if it's anachronistic to sing it on an album of nineteenth-century balcony hymns when it hadn't yet received that tune officially.

SB: Fair catch. Look, the musical recordings, overall, range widely, though, right? From opera to jazz, from progressive rock to folk and most genres in between.

VFT: Yeah. My personal favorite right now is Marcus Young's 2017 album *Pilgrim*. It's kind of a gospel-inflected, contemporary lounge jazz style with some thoughtful rapping framing the riffs on *The Pilgrim's Progress* as personal memoir and worship.

SB: Nice shout out. It's a world away from Vaughan William's opera but equally far from The Neal Morse Band's two double concept albums.

VFT: Tell Researcher a bit about their musical feel.

SB: Well, having said that, I guess their very adventurous progressive rock is a populist manifestation of the same melodrama that is associated with opera.

RES: Even if many opera buffs find Vaughan William's "Morality," as he called it, off-putting 'cos it doesn't have the romantic plot and musical devices of traditional opera.

SB: OK, so what I mean is that they can conjure the frenzied agony of temptation and fear of condemnation, and spiritual battle with bombastic melodic themes, phenomenal percussion and soaring electric guitar riffs.

VFT: But they're also musically diverse.

SB: Yes, they are. They also feature gospel singers as backing vocalists for an acoustic guitar led meditative song at the cross. And they're musically excellent. The album was a huge critical success in the Prog Rock world.

VFT: That last worship angle is a similar approach we see in album by The World in Lights called *Letter from a Bedford Jail*. It's built around narrative songs specifically on *The Pilgrim's Progress* and worship songs that slot in.

So the song "Messiah" stands in for the cross encounter in the sequence of the album although it's not a narrative account of that episode per se.

SB: And I love the way they then blend the old time hymn "I have decided to follow Jesus" as a theme behind some of their tracks that makes most poignant sense as the backing to Faithful's martyrdom at Vanity Fair.

VFT: The World in Lights, then, come in with an edgy variety of American folk, soft-rock, guitar led worship sound that is also represented by albums from Nate Currin and Jim Winders. This is recognizably Christian music in the broad flow of the Contemporary Christian Music movement since the 1980s.

SB: And I want to say that the breadth of musical style is fitting. The singing in Bunyan's book is religious but also popular—celebration, joy at good company, even bragging of vindication and the downfall of enemies. It's as much the stuff of sports stadium crowd chants as it is of churchly choirs, wouldn't you say?

VFT: Yes, and sometimes music gets to a simplicity of response, emotionally, that words, even as bare lyrics, cannot convey.

SB: Let's just quickly mention kid's music. It is less complex musically, while not being any less musical. So the children's choir record, *Enchanted Journey*, provides simplicity in spades, just take the "I'm Happy" song at the cross!

VFT: Don't mock, just remember that at the cross, Christian is happy, so the adaptation is not wrong!

SB: That's right, he's jumping for joy, literally!

VFT: Right, so for kids, repeating "I'm happy!" in association with the good news of the cross may not be as theologically articulate as other lyrics, but, at the same time, it is not a musical mistake, nor a betrayal of Bunyan in that instance.

SB: Elsewhere things are different: Some exemplars of *The Pilgrim's Progress* in music don't go beyond a nod of appropriation. 1970s band Procul Harum sing a track with the book title, but the lyrics merely borrow the conceit of a dreamer setting about one piece of writing and then finding thoughts going in another direction. A nod to Bunyan's "Author's Apology," for sure, but not substantively an adaptation. Likewise, multiple single songs take Pilgrim's Progress as a title or inspiration but have little reference to the narrative.

VFT: Isn't it enough to use Pilgrim's Progress as a title to suggest it is Pilgrim's Progress that is the stirring component of the music?

SB: Good question. I'd say that it can be hard to discern the connection of some instrumental pieces to the book precisely because they are not lyrically tied down. So, a Christian jazz-funk band called Koinonia have an instrumental track entitled "Pilgrim's Progression" in their 1984 album *Celebration*. Surely their confession means this is a knowing nod to Bunyan, but little more can be said about its place in the Pilgrimverse.

VFT: Even less certainty might attach to the similarly entitled track by the Dave Brubeck Quartet with Paul Desmond, on their *Newport 1958* album. There is definitely a sound journey over the course of the nearly ten-minute track, but as purely instrumental it would be hard to ascribe the movement of the piece to elements of Bunyan's story, still less his theology.

SB: OK, so if there are definitely some precursors, I still think we should chat about Greg Tardy's jazz suite called *The Journey*, don't you?

VFT: Yes, this piece gets us back from the electric instrumentation to the classical instruments, if that's the right term?

SB: Go on.

VFT: Tardy explicitly draws from Bunyan's book to tell the story of *The Pilgrim's Progress* in instrumental jazz form. It is orchestrated yet with space for improvisation. In the performance recorded *Live at Lucille's* in Knoxville, Tennessee, for PBS, "songs" within the suite are introduced by a narrator reading an adaptation of key episodes in the book.

SB: Sometimes those narrations get instrumental accompaniment as well, with some comic timing. This ensures that the absence of lyrics is not a lack. Rather the articulation of the music is framed by the narrative build up.

VFT: So, for example, the energy of Christian's consternation and flight from the City of Destruction in the first, fast, trumpet-led movement "The City of Destruction. What Must I do?" is paced differently to "The Cross" movement. This latter is gentler. It is flute-led with piano accompaniment and has interwoven snippets of echoes of familiar hymn melodies. "The Cross" crescendos as strings join in and, as the narrator promised, the music captures the "freedom and peace" of the release from Christian's burden.

SB: And then, do you remember? The collective improvisation at the beginning and end of the Vanity Fair movement perfectly captures the chaos of Bunyan's "hubbub" and the scandal of Faithful's trial and execution.

VFT: Oh, so good, yes!

RES: I hear you guys suggesting that, whether instrumental or lyrical, it is the multi-track works that lean deeper into their shaping by Bunyan's book. Does that mean that in order for *The Pilgrim's Progress* to stir the emotions musically the connection as adaptation has to be clearly foregrounded narratively?

SB: I think so, otherwise the tribute to the book in a title seems merely appropriative.

VFT: But, isn't even that a Pilgrimverse success story?

SB: How so?

VFT: Well, only that this deliberately dissenting, non-institutional, non-elite book for the people is even and still referenced in the popular and secular, even, at times, rebellious musical genres of jazz, funk, and pop?

SB: I suppose you could make the case that although the drive of Bunyan's classic is an escape from worldliness to the world to come, on another level of its art, it is a celebration of story-telling for the age of now, the secular rather than the eternal age. Maybe that good can be captured musically even if short of proclaiming the eternal dimension the book points to as its destination.

VFT: And therefore, its musical adaptation need not be restricted to congregational Sunday hymn singing or the contemporary worship genre, even though that is a fitting home, to be sure.

SB: Right, and as a matter of fact, as we've been hearing, it hasn't been.

VFT: There's more out there, but I think we've covered at least a representative range of Pilgrimverse sounds for you, Mr Researcher.

RES: Yes, you certainly have. Thank you so much. Why don't you guys chill and listen some more, without having to take notes—I hope that will be more relaxing.

VFT: We will, let's go see if we can find Faithful and Hopeful to share some of these sounds with them.

Shepherd boy and Mr Valiant-for-truth, happily getting along a lot better than when they'd first appeared, headed off to find their friends. At that, in my dream, I, Narrator, spoke out to Researcher.

NAR: So what do you make of these different ways that the Pilgrimverse has captured and adapted *The Pilgrim's Progress* in sound, Researcher?

RES: Hi, there, Narrator. I guess I know which products I could enjoy, but that seems mostly to do with my particular tastes in music.

NAR: There are some objective criteria in relation to production values that can rank some products as technically superior to others. A lot of that has to do with budget and the possibility to employ professionals for all aspects of the work.

RES: It's also somewhat cultural. All the listening we've tracked has been in English or with Western structures of sound and story-telling.

NAR: But if your boys had ventured further that might have found that, for example, Brazilian rock worship group, Banda Return's track "O Progresso do Peregrino" is a parallel to the Neil Morse Band end of the musical spectrum, while singer-songwriter and Pastor, Marco Telles's song, "Peregrino," charts the contemporary worship sounds in musical similarity with Currin and The World in Lights. These artists clearly track with the plot and theological motivation of *The Pilgrim's Progress*.

RES: That's interesting to hear of the Pilgrimverse from Brazil.

NAR: Well, let's offer a Brazilian contrast. For example, Dallyson Fernandes and Bruninho Music sing a bass-led dance track, "Peregrino," which confesses pilgrimage to heaven to embrace Jesus in love. It's a good instance of where the Pilgrimverse is not substantially in play, and we see that the use of the word for "pilgrim" need not have any clear Bunyan reference. The biblical basis for the image might be sufficient. But, and here's a challenge at the margins of the Pilgrimverse that we'll get to properly in the next expedition, you can still see the common vision that offers a Pilgrimverse parallel in the track's video. It shows a car passing through a dark "wilderness" of electricity pylons, followed by a space-suited pilgrim running through a haunted jagged wall of cold crystal up to a brightly lit cross. I think that all this shows is that Bunyan's imagery is scripturally inspired rather than there being a direct influence of the Pilgrimverse on the videographers.

RES: Wow, you've done a bit of digging while we were chatting?

NAR: You didn't think I did anything apart from dreaming, did you?

RES: Let's just move on.

NAR: OK, but first back to that familiarity of Western musicality, which still covers the Brazilian example. Even those tunes you enjoyed the least follow canonical patterns of chord progression or note scale so that, in some way, you can tell what's going on.

RES: Yes. Although Tardy's Jazz composition is, by genre, more improvisational and even rebellious musically, its story-telling works in relation to standard patterns of beat and melody.

NAR: This is interesting because it suggests that we are dealing with a language of music that is not reducible to lyrics.

RES: Right. So bizarre as it may be that jazz trios or rock groups or country bands take up *Pilgrim's Progress* in their track titles, they still participate in the Pilgrimverse as tributes to the endurance of the book title's presence.

NAR: And I think it would be too hasty to expel these from the Pilgrimverse because they did not pursue Bunyan's religious aims, or even, on some judgments, were aligned with the kind of worldliness he would eschew.

RES: Say more.

NAR: Well, just as there's a poetic rhythm to Bunyan's prose in places, and just as he employs verse to lift the expression of his writing above the simply mundane prose, we could suppose that in these ways he participates in a spiritual expression of creativity that is very much part of a creaturely good under God. Not infallibly, but humanly. So a good turn of phrase, or an amusing joke, while not spiritually indicating the riches of salvation in Jesus Christ, nevertheless showcase the good which is to be redeemed in him.

RES: So, you're saying that Bunyan's populist style and rough, preachy technique is a participation in the good of a world being redeemed.

NAR: Right, and without needing to claim to be directly divinely inspired or an authoritative guide to Christian living.

RES: Ok, but many Christians have found the book helpful in their spiritual walk, right?

NAR: And most likely, due to its structure as articulate prose promoting a Christian narrative of conversion and salvation, this will be more clearly the case for Bunyan than for Vaughan Williams's opera.

RES: Sure.

NAR: But it does not need to be the case in all instances. That is, it could be that Vaughan Williams's composition or The World in Lights' album participate in the good of music-making that encourages a listener in a way reading the book just doesn't.

RES: Music can reach parts words alone can't, you mean?

NAR: Not magically, as a bypass of reason, but as a participation in the reason that is constituted musically by the rationale of sound to which some are more attuned, and by which some are more emotionally affected than others.

RES: And not just emotionally, surely? I mean, couldn't it be that a good is served by the physiological stimulation that gets me tapping my feet, or even dancing.

NAR: I think that's right. If we as creatures are made to praise our creator, and if that praise can and is expressed musically in song, then this is a creaturely bodily performance. Surely singing is posture and attitude as much as physical movement of the larynx and tongue. So why not admit the whole body into that expressive equation?

RES: So if a pop song vaguely titled after Pilgrim's Progress leads me to a freedom to be human, even if unacknowledged by me and even the artist, before God, so much the better for that music.

NAR: Sure. And we can still affirm that Bunyan would himself want no one caught up in the artistry of music just as he didn't in relation to his writing in missing the gospel message he wants to communicate.

RES: Yet, also, the gospel message can find its auxiliary in the bodily stirring in hope or tension or even love that music inspires, invites or directs.

NAR: I trust in the Spirit that this could be so. As with all such claims, it is not just the punctual, immediate, even ecstatic experience that would prove this but also the life transformation to the way of Christ that bears fruit over time.

RES: Any of these hearing and listening encounters within the Pilgrimverse could open up the one with ears to hear to a transforming call to repentance and loyalty to God in Christ as *The Pilgrim's Progress* may make God known. But as with all human participations in the divine mission, hardened hearts and aesthetic pride, elitism or populism or any other mode of criticism could easily stand in the way.

NAR: Which brings us back to the verses at the beginning of this chapter. Music can elicit and warm hearts that are opened wide to others and the truth. Harmony, spiritually speaking, is a good of mission, but that harmony cannot ultimately be a conjunction of the discordant and clashing sounds of opposing eternal orientations. At the same time, short of that eternal judgment, this-worldly making of music and song can testify to an open-hearted participation in the goods of creation in such a way that those who enjoy or employ such music may do so to the glory of God, irrespective of or in subversive and cheerful opposition to the convictions or intentions of the human creators. This is especially true in music of instrumental form whose shape is open to interpretation, even as its reception will be governed by judgments about the goods of those places or people in which or among whom it prevails in popularity.

RES: Still, no musical genre need be beyond the pale of open-hearted listeners, don't you think?

NAR: As with all things, the kinds of judgments about products we've explored in this expedition report will be made on a case-by-case basis. This is the stirring soundscape of the Pilgrimverse.

Pilgrimverse Resources:

Banda Return. "O Progresso do Peregrino." From *Proteção*, 2009. Brazil. https://www.youtube.com/watch?v=uA_W4HuNzPY.

Bunyan, John, and David Shaw-Parker. *The Pilgrim's Progress. Complete Classics. Unabridged*. Potters Bar, UK: Naxos Audiobooks, 2013.

Currin, Nate. *The Pilgrim*, Archaic Canon Records, 2013.

Floria, Cam and Cher. *The Enchanted Journey: A Musical Adventure in the Land of Pilgrim's Progress*. Performed by "His Kids" of First Baptist Church, Pomona, CA. Compassion Radio. Special Re-Release CD. 1977.

Maddy Prior with the Carnival Band. "Who Would True Valor See." From *Sing Lustily & With Good Courage*, Say Disc, 1990.

Bunyan, John. *The Pilgrim's Progress*. Read by Max McLean. Grand Rapids: Zondervan, 2007.

Music, Bruninho, and Dallyson Fernandes. "Peregrino." May 20, 2022. https://www.youtube.com/watch?v=TAg52xHtOLM.

The Neal Morse Band. *The Similitude of a Dream*. Radiant Records, 2016.

Newton, John, [and Cowper, William]. *Olney hymns, in Three Books*. London: W. Oliver; J. Buckland; and J. Johnson, 1779.

Pappas, Jim. *Pilgrim's Progress Audio Drama Part 1*. Dobbins, CA: Orion's Gate, 2018.

Sibley, Brian *The Pilgrim's Progress: A Full-Cast BBC Radio Dramatization*. BBC Radio 4, Jan. 4, 2004. Audible audio ed., Nov. 16, 2023, 2 hrs., 51 mins.

Tardy, Greg. "The Journey." *Live at Lucille's: Great Performances from the World of Jazz*. PBS. Dec. 30, 2023.

Telles, Marco. "Peregrino." From *Devir*, 2019. https://www.youtube.com/watch?v=Kj9tBcoRQig.

Vaughan Williams, Ralph. *The Pilgrim's Progress: A Morality*. Opera, first performed at the Royal Opera House, Covent Garden, Apr. 26, 1951.

Vaughan Williams, Ralph. *The Pilgrim's Progress. Complete Radio-Play with Incidental Music*. BBC, Sept. 5, 1943. Adapted by Edward Sackville-West. Albion Records, 2015.

Winder, Jim, *The Hard But Right Way*. Notebook Records, 2001.

The World in Lights. *Letter from a Bedford Jail*. Digital download. 2016. https://www.theworldinlights.com/letter-from-a-bedford-jail.

Young, Marcus. *Pilgrim*. BLSSD Music, 2017.

7

Sights

> It was majestic in beauty,
> with its spreading boughs,
> for its roots went down
> to abundant waters.
>
> Ezekiel 31:7

I saw in my dream that Researcher was sat at his desk, scrolling on his smart phone. It wasn't settled reading, but flitting, as if he was grabbed by the images just as much as or more so than the headlines he clicked on. How much could he be taking in with such visual saturation?

As if shaking himself from the spell cast from the small hand-held device, he shook his head and pushed up his glasses to rub his eyes. He looked expectant. He must have been killing time, waiting for some more explorers to help with his project.

RES: Anyone else around to help me?

It was about that time of day this his *Pilgrim's Progress* friends had made a habit of joining him. There was still much to explore in the Pilgrimverse so he was hoping their portal-traveling abilities would speed up the next theme focus for him.

As providence would have it, he didn't have long to wait before two characters emerged from behind a pile on his desk, already deeply engaged in conversation. In fact, it seems they were having a minor disagreement.

The tall woman in a long white gown was saying, in a gentle Northern Irish accent: I don't see why you have a problem with it? Is it because I don't have a hat?

Her companion, a more roughly dressed man, replied: I'm just not calling you that. It's not dignified!

Interpreter (for this was her name): It's just an abbreviation—from Interpreter to Intty—pronounced with soft "t"s. It kind of sounds right for an adventure, don't you think? Intty? Indy? huh, Mr Porter?

Watchful (for this was his name) angrily retorted: You know I'm not *that* Watchful! He's the porter at the Palace Beautiful who guides Christian between the chained lions. I'm one of the Shepherds from the Delectable Mountains.

INT: What is it with the shepherds getting to explore so much? Shepherd boy was out and about exploring just a little earlier.

WAT: Well, he's the singing, David-like shepherd type. We on the other hand, that's me and my colleagues named Knowledge, Experience, and Sincere, we are more like the spiritual shepherds, known today as pastors, who teach the flock or the church. So, it's not really like we're from the same character category.

INT: Fair enough.

WAT: Anyway, I suspect the two of us are both here because we're all about vision. Is that right, Mr Researcher? Nice to meet you, by the way.

RES: That is right, Watchful. Hello, er, Indy.

INT: Thank you. Relax. It's just a bit of fun role play. As you know, I love conjuring up scenarios and painting pictures with words. You want us to help you explore how *The Pilgrim's Progress* has filled the Pilgrimverse with illustrations and visual representations, is that right?

RES: That's exactly right. You don't need to worry about graphic novels, as we have already been there, but Faithful and Hopeful only really dipped their toes in the visual Pilgrimverse. I hope you both will have more stamina.

WAT: I'm up for it. We shepherds are always showing pilgrims around, warning and encouraging them, and giving them glimpses of the Celestial City through our telescope, which Bunyan called a "perspective glass."

INT: And my house is the starting point for pilgrims who come through the Wicket Gate. But as I'm nearly always busy at home, it is good to get out and about, I must say.

RES: We should note that your character is often taken to be a personification of the Holy Spirit who leads into truth. Does that not defeat the purpose of an exploration?

INT: My self-understanding is that I'm here as narrative character only, the allegorical and spiritual realities intended or not by Bunyan aren't giving me an advantage here, I don't think.

RES: Well, OK then. You'll find visual reception of *The Pilgrim's Progress* in every corner of the Pilgrimverse. Where will you start?

WAT: Without being facetious, why don't we start with maps? It's just what we shepherds do.

INT: I'm down. Let's go!

    Quite a few book-covers sported maps of Christian's journey, and other maps could be found on the desk, but Watchful wanted to dig around to find an interesting portal entry so he pushed up the covers of some of the older books until he came across a couple with fold-out maps bound into the pages.

WAT: Which one would you like to jump through as a portal, Interpreter?

INT: Indy. Let me have a look. . . . I'm going to have to choose the black and white three panel vertical map, "A Plan of the Road from the City of Destruction to the Cœlestial City Adapted to the PILGRIM'S PROGRESS."

WAT: Any particular reason? I'd have thought you'd have liked the color spiral map in George Virtue's "Elegant Edition."

INT: I like the color. I do. And I like that both maps are composite illustrations of elements of both Part I and Part II. Do you see how they mark the spot where Simple, Sloth and Presumption are asleep after the cross in Part I, and a marker to the same spot from the other side of the road on the map indicates where they were hanged.

WAT: That's a bit grim.

INT: But I don't like the Virtue map, because, given my penchant for truth, I don't like misrepresentation. And here in this book, or as reproduced on the cover of the 2008 Penguin Classics edition, this map shows Christian, waist deep in the water of the River of Death, arms thrown up in despair, being helped by another person who has their arms around him. And the map has a label saying that "Evangelist saves Christian," but if you know the book at all, you know Evangelist doesn't appear after warning the pilgrims about Vanity Fair. It is Hopeful who helps Christian across, with a vision of Jesus sustaining the struggler. In fact, this very episode is captured delightfully by Justin Rowe's book art sculpture of that very scene, entitled: *Hopeful had much ado to keep his brother's head above water.*

WAT: Wow, I can tell that we're picking up Pilgrimverse vibes just by standing by the maps.

RES: These portals seem to be getting more potent. That might mean we're on limited time.

WAT: Let's be off then. Soonest departed, soonest returned! Do you agree, Indy?

At Indy's nod of assent, both of them jumped together, as it were, through the map, into the hidden dimensions of the Pilgrimverse. They were barely gone before they re-emerged, but not from their starting portal. They came up through the map on the cover of the "Triumphant Journey" 1000-piece jigsaw puzzle box.

WAT: So, Indy, you probably can't cope with the typo on the "Triumphant Journey" puzzle, can you? Where a caption says that Christian comes to Mt Sanai rather than Sinai.

INT: Aaaaaarrrrrgggggghhhhh!

WAT: Hold on a minute. About this truth thing? May I point out that you are a woman?

INT: What of it?

WAT: Well, that's hardly true to Bunyan's original.

INT: I see you lie at the catch.

WAT: What?

INT: It's a Bunyan way of saying that you're trying to catch me out. And fair enough. I'm only a woman in one version of *The Pilgrim's Progress* that I've seen in the Pilgrimverse. But it's got pretty wide attention. It's the

Sights

Revelation Media 2019 CGI movie directed by Robert Fernandez. My voice is Kristyn Getty's. And, what's more, I reckon that the importance of the Bible in the Pilgrimverse is only boosted by this casting: Kristyn Getty now voices the audio of the ESV Bible app!

WAT: Duly noted. But back to the puzzle. Let me point out that, apart from a typo, it is well designed and produced, entertainingly illustrated, and faithfully covering major narrative episodes. Tellingly, it comes with a ten-page booklet with a key. Each enumerated label on the map is explained in a little more detail in connection with the plotted episode, as well as being accompanied by a Bible verse to support the truth taught.

INT: So even here, we see that the good of the artistic visual expression serves as illustrative handmaiden to the message of the written word.

WAT: At the same time, the fun of jigsaw puzzle-solving comes in the construction of the image itself to the satisfaction of the puzzle solver: it's a tactile and visual fit, rather than a conceptual one, at the end of the day.

INT: That's right, so we need to be careful in not suggesting too rigid an ordering of the visual to written in the Pilgrimverse.

WAT: You mean, as if visual was necessarily inferior to the written? Exactly, I reckon that the breadth of visual artistry across editions of *The Pilgrim's Progress* testifies to the importance and even the attraction of image alongside the word.

INT: That's certainly going to be the case in the instance where the edition is prepared for children.

RES: Let me redirect you there, we've already come across the children's adaptations in the home themed expedition.

WAT: Ok, but, with all due respect, we might need to revisit the terrain with our exclusive focus on the visual, if that's All right?

RES: Sure, I'll just have Narrator look out for, and head off, any repetition. OK?

NAR: OK, happy not to be forgotten up here. I'm glad you acknowledge I'm keeping this whole show on the road, in any case.

RES: That's not quite what I said.

INT: *Go with Christian* is the most obviously visually participative of book versions.

INTO THE PILGRIMVERSE

NAR: Already covered in the Pilgrimverse home expedition.

INT: Well, hear me out. The details are telling, and I've a personal investment in this one: It's a pop-up book that also has pull tabs and liftable inserted pages. The pull-out Interpreter's House page has windows as tabs that open up, advent calendar style, to reveal images and accompanying Bible verses. But here's where some of the incongruity of the image and the message is seen. There's a figure of a woman brushing up dust behind one of those tab windows. If this were to correspond to Bunyan's original we'd expect it to say something about God's grace cleaning the heart where the law cannot. Instead, the accompanying phrase and Bible reference is: "Work hard at whatever you do. Ecclesiastes 9:10."

WAT: Right, it takes a particularly prooftexty approach to Ecclesiastes to take a book proclaiming that all is vanity, as Bunyan was very aware, and use it to promote obedient children's chore fulfilment!

INT: That's my feeling, too.

WAT: But, don't you think that, in a way, any adaptation for small children, just because of scope and understanding, is always going to be selectively prooftexty about which bits of *The Pilgrim's Progress* it is going to offer and illustrate? And, what's more, if illustration serves to draw extra attention to what now are assumed to be key episodes, even illustration of the full text will apportion importance disproportionately on the scenes illustrated rather then those left unadorned.

INT: Let's stick with the children's adaptations just a little longer. What's fun about *Go with Christian!* as a visual product is that it also participates in a trajectory of treatments for different ages by the same artist. Not only did Alan Parry illustrate this edition, but also, in collaboration with his wife Linda, he provided the images for an animal character adaptation short chapter book named *The Evergreen Wood*, or sometimes *The Progress of Pilgrim Mouse* in the US. For slightly older readers or as a read aloud with pictures on every page, that was more of a Beatrix Potter like treatment.

WAT: One detail stood out for me from the *Evergreen Wood* illustrations. Most delightfully, for capturing a glimpse of Bunyan's theology, Christopher Mouse, having been instructed by Brockley Badger, reaches a path with a wall on every side. This is the parallel to the place of deliverance and the cross and tomb in *The Pilgrim's Progress* where Christian loses his burden. Well, Christopher loses his burden too, but not in seeing a cross, but in meeting a white lamb!

RES: That's brilliant, to capture a theology of Jesus as the atonement sacrifice for sin like that!

INT: I thought so!

WAT: A recent version of the animal characterization is also offered in a slight altering of Helen Taylor's 1883 *The Little Christian's Pilgrimage* which has mutated over the decades to be known as *Little Pilgrim's Progress*. Sticking to the woodland approach, here artist Joe Sutphin has rabbits and badgers and mice but "the good prince," who represents Jesus, is a Lion. Admittedly, this is ecologically incongruous. But, of course, this is both biblical for Jesus as the Lion of Judah, and Narnia-eque after C. S. Lewis's Aslan. And it represents the other obvious animal option, aside from Parry's lamb, for depicting the one who has died on the cross.

INT: Sutphin's choice also provides a fun embodiment of eschatological hope in fulfilment of prophecy because Taylor, in her adaptation, makes the first picture in the Interpreter's House about the Good Shepherd having rescued the lost sheep. In Bunyan's original the man looking up to heaven, although sometimes read as Jesus, is more readily interpreted as a godly pastor in the model of the apostle Paul. But by making him Jesus, Taylor allows Sutphin to then create a sweet image of an anthropomorphized Lion holding a lamb in his arms.

WAT: Too cute! But, let's just go back to Alan Parry, because he also illustrates Oliver Hunkin's adaptation *The Dangerous Journey*. This is an interesting project because it emerged from a Yorkshire TV production in the UK. The TV show consisted of Hunkin's narrative text read over shots of the camera panning over Parry's artwork. Then we get the tie-in book. We see the versatility of Parry's artistic skill in his adult characters in period setting. The depictions of Apollyon, the Valley of the Shadow of Death, and Giant Despair's castle boneyard are on the scary side but there's also a grostequery in depicting unsympathetic characters that is humorous.

INT: I like it that Parry, in all his versions, has Christian armed for his battle with Apollyon but otherwise, in all other scenes, he is simply dressed in regular clothing. Many versions take a greater delight in the military glory of Christian's armor such that he wears it from the Palace Beautiful onwards all the way to the Celestial City, whereas Bunyan's text never mentions it after the Valley of the Shadow of Death, relatively early in the narrative.

RES: Yes, you've spotted ways in which illustrators are subtly adding their own interpretations and shaping the interpretation of readers with "paratext."

INT: Christian wears this armor through to the end of Robert Fernandez's movie (even though the director and producer comment in a podcast that they regret not having more footage of him in his new raiment after the cross!).

WAT: This is a good example of the influence of prior illustration constraining judgments that are not warranted by the text being illustrated and adapted. But this is stock representation of a militaristic Christian through the nineteenth century as well. It endures through to editions today in illustrations of Jean Watson's *Family Pilgrim's Progress* or Rousseaux Brasseur's poetic retelling or, and in educational versions produced by Great Commission Publications, or Answers in Genesis.

RES: Should we suppose that some Christian groups, being more militant in their expression of faith render Christian triumphalistically in the nineteenth and combatively as a culture warrior in the twenty-first centuries, according to their own self-understanding?

INT: That could be it, but also it could just be, more innocently, a repetition of an imaginative formula that goes unquestioned as an interpretation of the text, even if it turns out to be an interpretation of a silence in the text.

WAT: But the stock knightly image of Christian is not the only way to picture the text. This most notable in the greater detail afforded to Alan Parry by the *Dangerous Journey* edition. Here Parry shows that Christian's breastplate is held on merely by thin leather straps at his back, confirming Bunyan's claim that Christian could not safely turn his back on the monster and flee. And once the battle with Apollyon is done, Christian is seen venturing into the Valley of the Shadow of Death with only a sword.

INT: Beatriz Mello's illustrations for Tyler Van Halteren's children's adaptation, *Little Pilgrim's Big Journey*, keeps to that same costuming detail, this time rendered on child characters. The armor is only for the battle with Apollyon.

WAT: So, although armor is a dominant way of dressing Christian in visual reception it's not the only way.

INT: In fact, Gerta Norvig's extensive study of William Blake's iconic illustrations of *The Pilgrim's Progress* makes a similar kind of point. Although these never actually found their way into a book in the artist's lifetime that have been collated in fancy collectors' editions in the last century, most recently with an updated Folio edition.

RES: That's the most expensive book I own!

NAR: And it's too big and heavy to read!

RES: But it is beautiful, nonetheless!

INT: As I was saying, Norvig claims that illustrators have tended to approach *The Pilgrim's Progress* with the battle with Apollyon as the creative centerpiece of their work.

WAT: And so it was Blake's depiction of that scene that was on the cover of the Penguin Classics edition for a while.

INT: Quite so. But Norvig says that Blake's double depiction of the Cross and the Shining Ones rightly form the center piece of his production on Bunyan's classic. That is, the artist points his reader to a much more irenic, that is, peaceful visual tribute to pilgrimage and spiritual growth in Christ.

WAT: A different approach than that of high art, as Blake would now be categorized, is found in Rhoda Couldridge's *Christian's Journey* which is illustrated by her young daughter, Anna. The drawings, in color, have flat human characters in a range of simple postures.

RES: These have been critiqued as amateurish, but I remember reading this copy when I was little, and I found the pictures immediately compelling as they were the kind of visual images I could imagine myself to have done. I was drawn in with sympathy to the visual presentation in a way which more accomplished adult illustrations could not achieve.

INT: Well said. You help us remember that illustration is not just about beautifying according to canons of art, but is about generating affective engagement with the story.

WAT: Did you say effective, with an "e"?

INT: No, I said, affective, with an "a." I mean that the spectacle of meeting illustration strikes the eye of the heart as much or sometimes more so than of the mind.

RES: The use of illustration in children's books is tried and tested, of course, not only to draw them into the story but also into the participation in reading itself.

WAT: You've got to think that Bunyan would approve, given the importance he and his Protestant community put on reading, especially the Bible.

INT: So we should recognize, however much variety we found, and there is a lot, that illustration is constrained by the text illustrated.

RES: Absolutely. And Bunyan would love that, too. After all, it's in encountering an image that they cannot immediately decipher that Hopeful, in the text, calls on Christian's superior learning and reading skill. He, the better reader, has to work out from an inscription, that the pillar they come across is a statue of Lot's wife, from Genesis 19.

INT: It's a little hard, reporting to you in your time, Mr Researcher, to capture the power of older images in the Pilgrimverse. Today many of the nineteenth-century line drawings and lithographs look austere and dull, but that might be more so due to our context of near total visual saturation. It may not fairly represent reader response at the time.

WAT: We might at least infer that the continued production of ever more greatly illustrated editions was a response to popularity of the product, especially of the illustrations.

INT: At the same time, the re-use of centuries-old illustrations in many editions of the twenty-first century, while honoring of the book's legacy, seems to miss the opportunity of engaging creativity in today's terms for the sake, dare I say it, of easily reproduced work now out of copyright?

WAT: Visual renderings of *The Pilgrim's Progress* often seek to capture Bunyan's historical context by reproducing seventeenth-century dress, even if this is then mixed with medieval armor, to reproduce an original faithfulness.

INT: Some will move figures even further back into stock images sliding over from Bible illustration. Or rather, they use the same costuming as is being used for Bible illustrations. This makes sense, for example, for H. C. Selous's Shepherd-boy in Part II, as he's a figure of the young King David, in any case. But I'm not so sure about the medieval being cast back into biblical visual references for Christian and Hopeful. I suppose, besides taste, I'll grant that there's something to this ploy, given Bunyan's own dependence on the Bible.

WAT: But another move is to adapt the visuals of the story to contemporary settings. Barry Moser's illustrations of Gary D Schmidt's book are rendered in vibrant color. Moser depicts a baseball cap wearing Christian in red shirt and blue jeans navigating industrial scale fields of wheat.

INT: It's also fun to see Moser turn the tables on those traditional readings. This is done poignantly in Schmidt's book, as evangelist is first introduced in the text as a man "neither young nor old . . . his beard was white, but his gait was quick, his hands smooth and strong on the staff he carried lightly" The full-page image of Evangelist only comes in the book at his third appearance, when he meets Christian and Faithful before they enter Vanity, many pages later.

WAT: It's only then that we see Evangelist as a white-bearded black man dressed in white suit with red tie and matching pocket square. This is striking, if we recall that the only black figure of the illustration tradition, drawing directly from Bunyan's own text, is the Flatterer. And, in the person of the Flatterer, black skin is a placeholder for devilish evil.

RES: I argue elsewhere that this racially problematic depiction by Bunyan and subsequent artists of the Flatterer has made *The Pilgrim's Progress* a "white" text in some communities of Christians.

INT: Good. To my mind, there's no doubt that an assumption of Evangelist's whiteness is in conformity with the illustrative tradition and this makes Moser's Evangelist a surprise.

WAT: The original artwork of that illustration from Schmidt's retelling of *Pilgrim's Progress* is on display Moser's Penny Royal Press website.

RES: Sadly, I can't afford it.

INT: What about this? I suspect a similar gentle subversion of racial hierarchies is at play in the Lithos Kids' publication of *Little Pilgrim's Big Journey*. Beatriz Mello depicts the Interpreter in that series as a white haired, old-aged Asian man, in conservative traditional dress.

WAT: Instead of bucking traditions, new illustrations can also revisit older visual effects. Moser does this with his assorted close-up facial portraits, which mimic the oft-reprinted images of a similar type from the nineteenth century.

INT: Similarly, Joanna Troughton's black and white line drawings for James Reeve's re-telling evoke older woodcut traditions. I think you've seen similar black and white illustration in graphic novels.

RES: We did.

NAR: Maybe I should point out here that woodcuts are images created by carving a block of wood so that the desired lines and shapes of an illustration are raised in relief. This allows the raised surface to take the ink that then can be pressed onto paper. Later technologies use copper plates or lithographs, where the design is impressed with the substance used to draw on the stone or plate reacting to ink while water keeps the unused spaces on the stone or plate clean for the printing to take. Eventually printing images directly will mimic photography and then digital arts.

WAT: Let's pay some attention to those original woodcut designs, shall we? They certainly set a trajectory of illustration in the Pilgrimverse, but we don't know who the artists behind the images are. Only in 1728 does credit get given to William Sturt, and illustrators start to leave their mark, even as anonymous, publisher commissioned illustration carries on through the tradition.

INT: We've already mentioned the celebrated illustrations by William Blake, but the early woodcuts are much rougher productions. Simple designs, untroubled by perspective in capturing key moments of the journey.

WAT: What is illustrated is pretty significant. The earliest illustration, aside from a famous frontispiece by Robert White in the 3rd, came in the 4th edition. It was of Vanity Fair showing Faithful's execution. Thus that episode must have been understood by, and communicated to, readers as about political and religious persecution, rather than, say, a critique of capitalism.

INT: And Roger Pooley suggested that the curve of the blades in that illustration, and the elaborates headdresses, are meant to evoke the "Turk." If so, with scimitars waving, the illustration points to late seventeenth-century antipathy toward the Moorish or Barbary to be expected of the English nationalist readership.

WAT: This, in turn, could make the construction of the Flatterer as a man "Black of flesh" by Bunyan a nativist device and not just simply racist.

INT: Quite so.

WAT: It's fair to say that, slowly, and then with greater momentum, illustrations become more sophisticated and plentiful. They move from having to be separable inserted full-page woodcuts or engraved plates, to finding their way amidst the words of the book as vignettes—getting smaller and grabbing space on most pages.

INT: Eventually color printing technology will elevate a few expensive plates among the other black and white illustrations, until all the images can appear in color or on pages that are themselves colorful.

WAT: In that rush to abundance, scarcity starts to look sophisticated in response. This explains the visual appeal and curiosity of the Nonesuch Press 300th anniversary edition of 1928, limited to 1600 copies. German artist and designer, Karl Michel, uses the lines of modern art's minimalism to render a few celebratory woodcut illustrations: a version of the dreaming Bunyan frontispiece, the lions at Palace Beautiful, battle with Apollyon, caged pilgrims at Vanity, and the Shining One coming to help the pilgrims netted by the Flatterer.

INT: The other oddity of this prettily produced book is the paring of Part I to Bunyan's next creative prose writing, *The Life and Death of Mr Badman*, rather than with Part II, *Grace Abounding*, or even *The Holy War*, all of which have been far more popular pairings.

WAT: Editions seeking greater authenticity start to reverse the course of excessive, perhaps, vulgar representational illustration, with the reprinting of original woodcuts in recent Oxford World's Classics or Penguin Classics editions.

INT: And even in those editions, because of the variety even among editions, the Penguin images are more sophisticated in detail, produced, according to editor Roger Pooley, from Dutch engravings, than the Oxford images, purportedly the same. The images used by editor W. R. Owens are sourced from George Offor's nineteenth-century collation from earlier editions, but the lines are much thicker and there is far less detail in illustrations that copy the poses and setting of the Dutch engravings but to a much rougher effect.

INT: But are we saying that the early woodcut tradition of illustration endured through to niche anniversary publications of the 1920s then?

WAT: The overall picture makes it seem that woodcut illustrations have been gone for centuries, but, like the Nonesuch edition, as recently as the 1980s, the eccentric author and publisher E. L. Carr issued a sixteen-page string of extracts from Part I accompanied by commissioned woodcuts by Christopher Fiddes, one of Britain's last exponents of the craft. Fiddes is known for the social and political commentary of his art as well as the retrieval and preservation of neglected techniques, making him an interesting interpreter in the Pilgrimverse.

INT: And his last little illustration at the place of the celestial city shows the pilgrim leaning on his staff enveloped by the hands of a large, bearded figure filling the right of the image. The hair and beard blowing from right to left is evocative of William Blake's "Ancient of Days" and shows the persistence of a minority expression of socially critical and mystical illustration.

INT: Right, I guess that, because so much illustration is oriented to children, it can end up having a kind of cutesy styling that lacks some of Bunyan's combative edge.

WAT: Which Fiddes undoubtedly seeks to uncover.

INT: And then Carr's own cover art merges various sketches in mapping the journey of Part I starting with Bunyan's portrait at bottom center then moving anti-clockwise around a collage of images and labels to arrive back as bottom left at the Celestial City.

WAT: How about we move a little beyond illustration?

INT: Sure. Where do you want to go? The Pilgrimverse is envisioned in sculpture, woodcarving reliefs, and stained glass. The former is interesting, I think, in relation to the role of pillars and monuments as warnings and markers of triumph in Bunyan's text.

WAT: That's right, Christian and Hopeful erect a monument to warn pilgrims after they escape from Doubting Castle.

INT: And that's after they've taken warning from running into, not literally, a pillar of salt who turns out to be Lot's wife.

WAT: Yes. Don't look back to the attractions of Demas and his Silver mines of Lucre hill, Hopeful!

INT: Quite. Well, there's a guided meditation walk through the episodes of both Part I and Part II in the form of a sculpture garden in Pilgrim House, in Gyeonggi-do, South Korea.

WAT: The bronze statues reproduce Bunyan's characters with Asian physiognomies, except for the "Portrait of the Shepherd" which has a much more European face and the flowing wavy locks of hair more readily associated with Walter Sallman's blonde, nordic Jesus, even though, again, the image is in bronze relief.

INT: The Sculptures are accompanied with a guided audio tour to explain their place in the narrative, and even invite participation as, for example, Passion and Patience's seats at the Interpreter's House are left empty, inviting walking pilgrims to put themselves in the scene with discernment and perhaps not a little repentance!

WAT: The path itself leads appropriately to an ornate hospitality building, House Beautiful, with a café for refreshment, an exhibit peace room for quiet, an armory displaying the Armor of God, and an extensive library.

INT: Carved relief scenes of Part I also decorate the celebratory doors of the Bunyan Meeting church building in Bedford.

WAT: And they have their own stained-glass windows.

INT: As also, more bizarrely, do a few ecumenically minded Anglican churches, including London's Southwark Cathedral, no less.

WAT: Before we totally move on from wood-panelling, though, I've thought of a visual theme in adaptations along those lines. Hear me out. So, in the 2008 movie, *Journey to Heaven,* written and directed by Danny Carrales, the Interpreter's house is a mansion of sorts. Each of the gospel teaching "emblems" appear as a bright light behind wood panel doors from an equally fancy wood-paneled central hallway. In his 2019 movie, Robert Fernandez takes wood paneling to the next level by locating the Interpreter's House fully inside a tree. And, like Dr Who's TARDIS, it's way bigger on the inside than on the outside. In fact, once the Interpreter invites Christian through a door in the circular corridor, they leave spatial geography behind to float past massive, as it were, IMAX scale visions of the various visual parables that the Interpreter wants Christian to engage.

INT: Nice connection. There are other large images out there, right?

WAT: Right. Suzanne Miller produced a mural honoring literary classics that featured *The Pilgrim's Progress* in 1937 for the Long Beach Public Library, in Southern California. Her depiction is not tied slavishly to the tradition of illustration in that she uses vibrant color and modern, almost cartoonish, representation of figures and landscape. What she does introduce is a particularly American patriotic read of both the pilgrim and the progress.

RES: What do you mean by that?

INT: Well, the pilgrim is shown in the typical dress associated in the popular imagination with the New England Puritan pilgrims—tall black hat, wide white collars, and black clothing. The kind of thing you could snatch up for a kid's costume for Halloween and Thanksgiving rolled into one.

WAT: And what's more, she locates the pilgrim, the Lion and the looming Giant of her composite tribute to Bunyan on coastal cliffs, with a Mayflower-looking ship at sea on the horizon.

RES: So there's a conflation of Bunyan's England with America's own history and story of origin, right?

INT: Yes, and the most fun detail, surely a joke by the artist, is the small section of white picket fencing in the foreground of the mural panel.

WAT: I just thought of this. Is that a visual pun on wicket gate, do you think?

INT: I very much hope so!

RES: I love it. There's a more spiritually attuned mural in St Elisabeth's church in Eastbourne, Southern England, too. Did you come by it?

WAT: Yes we did. But it's no longer in the church crypt. The building was demolished in 2019.

RES: So where is it?

WAT: In storage. Perhaps a patron reading this book would find it a home?

RES: Tell us more.

INT: It is an impressive sweeping panorama of rare Holocaust Art that would have covered around 40 meters of the church crypt that was itself dedicated as a War Memorial in 1943. The muralist Hans Feibusch himself was a Jewish artist and refugee who had fled Nazi Germany to England. The work was a personal project, not commissioned, that fuses

Sights

Bunyan's classic with his own story of escape from destruction and toward hope.

WAT: The most striking scene, looked at in hindsight, is that of the gaunt figure sinking in the River of Death. It is hard to see the naked figure and not recall the images of emaciated Nazi concentration camp survivors liberated two years after the original composition.

RES: Thanks guys. Murals are just vulnerable, aren't they?

NAR: They are. We'll mention another designed by Melvin Patterson when we explore the Pilgrimverse margins, but, sadly, that's been painted over when the building that housed it was repurposed.

INT: That is a shame. But even before movies and before any murals we have record of there was mass visual culture in the Pilgrimverse. Do you remember that I mentioned the camera panning across Parry's illustrations of *The Dangerous Journey*? Well, that rolling across a static visual construction of *The Pilgrim's Progress* is much older than television.

RES: Tell us more.

INT: If you're into what you might call high art, cultured representational landscapes, for example, you'd be impressed by the scope and enterprise of the visual landscape produced as a "Moving Panorama." This is a 8-foot high and 800-foot long painting created in 1851 showcasing designs by luminaries of what is known as the Hudson River School of American landscape painting. In a theatre setting, each scene would be scrolled along before a seated audience of thousands, to the accompaniment of narration of a lecturer on the story of Pilgrim's Progress.. Several of these "Bunyan Tableaux" existed, but only this 1851 has survived. It played its opening run in New York for six months straight, with nearly two-thirds of the city's population paying for admission.

WAT: It toured for nearly thirty years! This was a box office success, making over $100,000 in its first year.

INT: These had popular cachet—it was like the cinema of its day—static pictures that moved. The only other magical equivalent visually would be the appropriately named Magic Lantern slides that consisted of painted or printed images on glass slides whose image would be projected by means of an oil lamp and later electrical lamp light. A precursor to the photographic film slide projectors, these would have toured Sunday School classes or accompanied missionaries in their travels.

INT: Some of those Magic Lantern slides are painted scenes from the book, but others are more like the later photographic film slides, they have printed photographic images on them, capturing actors depicting scenes from the book.

WAT: That's right! Faithful bound at the stake was a particularly melodramatic pose!

INT: Yes, very pious upturned gaze!

WAT: But at least the Lantern's don't overdo the horror of Faithful's death. Only one that we saw shows a smoking wood pile.

INT: Yes, if you want the full fiery graphics, the most horrific has to be on the number 7 card of the yellow-sun-on-red-background suit in Pepys series of playing cards. They have full flames consuming the whole lower half of Faithful's body as he experiences a grimacing anguish.

WAT: So there have been static images, of one sort or another, and moving ones, but we should also mention performances in the Pilgrimverse. Vaughan Williams's opera has been performed in tradition seventeenth-century garb, but also as a World War I affair set in the trenches.

INT: Or as a post-modern, kaleidoscopic dystopia for the royal Opera House in the early 2000s—all grotesque excess: the burlesque and carnivalesque set against an austere incarcerated wilderness of a world from which the pilgrim must escape.

WAT: Oh, and when it comes to visualizing the Pilgrimverse, and anticipating the gender conversation that Narrator told me is going to be going on when you explore the margins, there's a recorded performance of Nissi Company's *O Peregrino*, from Brazil, which actually tells the whole story of Part I as acted by a female protagonist, and therefore narrated as being about a "peregrina."

INT: Her name is Cristã, feminine, rather than Cristão, masculine.

WAT: And the fact that other recordings of the same play have a male protagonist indicates that the decision for a female Christian was not a polemical one but rather a casting one that nevertheless illustrates, if you'll pardon the pun, the secondary question of sex and gender for a twenty-first-century production's portrayal of salvation and discipleship, that may be at odds with Bunyan's.

INT: Sticking then with plays, how about the way in which a 2019 production of Kenneth Wright and Wayne Scott's musical theater adaptation plays on the allegorical conceit of the original.

WAT: Yes, that's one of the decisions I liked best. They find a great way to represent the in-your-face obviousness of Bunyan's allegorical names. Each actor wears a name-sign hanging around their neck. The Bunyan/Dreaming Narrator character dispenses these to the cast from his satchel as the play progresses.

INT: I love the ways in which artistic directors and set designers navigate the Pilgrimverse in staging their productions.

WAT: We haven't mentioned dance, as yet. If the cast of *The Pilgrim's Progress* Part I might be predominantly male, what happens when a youth ballet company perform an interpretation?

INT: Well, the only example we were privileged to watch a recording of is from the Fidèle Youth Dance Company, a Christian-led group from Colorado Springs, Colorado. Not only is it fascinating to see how the performance is staged and to what selections of music they dance, it is a prime example of adaptation to a genre and profile of performer that is well beyond the text.

WAT: The production augments Apollyon's costume to artificially extend his dragon-like profile beyond the dancer's body, one of only two boys in the company. But then they communicate Giant Despair's outsized threat of evil through manic dance and costume, not the stature of the dancer. It's very well done!

INT: Another interpretative move is to have the character of the Holy Spirit do what Bunyan in his text indicates, in the words of the Interpreter, is happening on Christian's journey all along: the Comforter is with her throughout the play from conversion onwards.

WAT: The director, Mimi McKinnis, notes that when the Holy Spirit and Christian share the stage, Christian's movements are imitative of the Spirit's but also momentarily lagging, as if learning from and imitating in real time.

RES: Wow, that's a insightful theological take to incorporate into dance!

WAT: I know! And if you've got a whole dance troupe, you are going to need to flood the stage at times. Some scenes, in the City of Destruction or Vanity Fair or reaching the Celestial City lend themselves to large group dance.

INT: One detail among many that I loved about the performance was the multiplying of Shining Ones at the cross so that Christian is attended beautifully by a whole heavenly host. The moment of transformation in losing her burden is wonderfully achieved as she is surrounded by a circle of Shining Ones, wings raised to form a curtain, as they step, en pointe, elegantly around her in circular movement.

WAT: Oh, talking of this group performance reminds me that I did want to mention its complete opposite.

RES: What do you mean?

WAT: I mean the Pilgrim's Progress one man show that is David Simpich's marionette theater performance. His theater building was shut down due to the double impact of storage flooding and COVID-19. But not before a recording had been made of the Pilgrim's Progress show.

RES: I'm thinking that this is performance on a very different scale, right?

WAT: Yes, the sets are a few feet high to accommodate the marionette dolls and Simpich's reach over them. With up to four puppets on stage at any one time, Simpich varies his voice in keeping with each character.

INT: It is intriguing to see how the puppeteer's bare hands float out from black-sleeved arms to mimic divine agency as they remove Christian's burden from his back at the Cross. Similarly, they equip him with the armor at Palace Beautiful—including with a key of promise—a version of the many ways visual adaptations try to have better continuity than Bunyan himself for Christian to them remember the key in Doubting Castle.

WAT: All the attractions of Vanity Fair are listed as Bunyan gives them, with the knowing addition of "puppet shows"!

RES: That was a fun little detail.

INT: Judge Hate-good and Vanity's jury are represented by mounted masks, again, seemingly floating sinisterly against the dark backdrop.

WAT: And just 'cos you noticed this in the graphic novels, once Faithful is dispatched, Hopeful replaces him, and is noticeably represented by a racially black puppet.

NAR: And we'll notice this again very soon, at the Pilgrimverse margins.

Sights

INT: It's worth noting that there is such variety in the sights of the Pilgrimverse because by definition, where the text is relatively fixed, the imagination of what the words might lead to in visual representation is not fixed at all in the same way.

WAT: So, back to book illustration, it's not uncommon for a publisher to keep a book in print while changing out the visual images. This is what happens with Little Pilgrim's Progress that has been published by Moody Press in the US since 1947 but undergone multiple revisions of illustrations. Moody stuck with the British line drawing illustrations by Scottish artist Lindsay Cable, which were themselves replacements of the original Victorian figural representations by H. J. A. Miles. Moody later drop Cable, and adopt images by Kelly Shields, that return to a more representational approach. That version is then eventually followed by a celebratory combination of Cable, Shields, and Joanne Brubaker's work, before most recently giving way to Joe Sutphin in the anthropomorphized animal update.

RES: Wow! So the text stays the same and yet the reading experience will vary according to the illustrations?

INT: Yep, same text for over one hundred years, until some slight tweaks for animals replacing children just a few years ago.

WAT: That's mostly with the same press, at least since 1947. The same kind of thing is true of Peter Wane's creative vision that gives a Terry Pratchett-esque-Discworld appearance to Jean Watson's *The Pilgrim's Progress* for its 1978 publisher, Scripture Union. The book illustration is a very rich fantasy/sci-fi genre visual experience. But, by 1983, the same publisher has moved on to use Vic Mitchell's more staid and figuratively representational illustrations. And it is Mitchell who gets the nod when Christian Focus take over the book title in 2007.

INT: It's all a matter of taste, but for me, Wane's images were much more creative, so it's a loss when they don't endure.

WAT: I did spot, by the way, that they were picked up by a Brazilian edition in 2004, though, so there's life in the Pilgrimverse for Wane's images beyond the original English language commissioning!

INT: Oh, good.

WAT: But it is also clear, examining the two English language books, that the way Wane is able to use the full double page spread, single page plates, vertical and horizontal panel settings of images is more demanding of a press than Mitchell's images which can be redistributed around different type settings with greater ease.

NAR: I sense you could all chat on forever, but we're going to have to wrap it up soon if there's to be one more expedition.

INT and WAT: Sorry.

RES: Don't apologize, guys. There's just so much to report. From maps to book covers and illustrations in their various technological guises, to marionettes and magic lanterns, to costumes, set designs, and even dance adaptations, there's just so much that can be appreciated and showcased as the sights of the Pilgrimverse.

NAR: Have we got you any nearer a comment on the opening verse, Mr Researcher?

RES: Well, this feels a little contrived, and its certainly not a comment on the verse in context but rather an extrapolation from its juxtaposition alongside our conversation. I'd say that there is much beauty in the Pilgrimverse. The roots of the varied Pilgrimverse sights are the original story but also the flowing waters of cultural and artistic influence. Of course, then, the visual expression of the Pilgrimverse if fluid, if you'll pardon the pun. Or, the boughs of the tree of the visual Pilgrimverse, so well-watered is the tree, spread exceedingly wide. The visual can stand alone, but is not far from the support of the text or its adaptation or a space of display or performance that affirms the goodness of Bunyan's vision in some way, whether religiously or simply as a cultural artefact of literary and historical inspiration.

NAR: I'm happy with that. We've nearly completed our survey of the Pilgrimverse, but there's territory at the margins that we have to check out. I'll meet up with you in a bit, Mr Researcher, to see that underway.

Pilgrimverse Resources mentioned in this expedition:

Collé, Nathalie. "Extra-Illustrating the Road: Fold-Out Maps as Material and Conceptual Add-Ons to John Bunyan's Pilgrim's Progress." *Journal of Illustration* 8:2 (2021) 187–219.

Hunkin, Oliver. *Dangerous Journey: The Story of Pilgrim's Progress*. Grand Rapids: Eerdmans, 1985.

Sights

Magic Lanterns: consult *either* Lucerna—The Magic Lantern Web Resource (https://lucerna.exeter.ac.uk/) *or* de Luikerwaal (https://www.luikerwaal.com/newframe_uk.htm?/pilgrim01_uk.htm).

McKinnis, Mimi, dir. *The Pilgrim's Progress*. Colorado Spring, CO: Fidèle Youth Dance Company, 2022.

Norvig, Gerda S. *Dark Figures in the Desired Country: Blake's Illustrations to "The Pilgrim's Progress."* Berkeley: University of California Press, 1993.

Oliveira, Caíque. O Peregrino. Cia de Artes Nissi. *O Peregrino*. Play performed at Igreja Batista em Renovação Espiritual, Ibrejetibá, July 23, 2023. https://www.youtube.com/watch?v=7-MHaGsrzrg

Parry, Alan, and Linda Parry. *The Evergreen Wood*. Nashville: Oliver Nelson, 1992.

"Pilgrim House Retreat Center." Gyeonggi-do, S. Korea. https://www.en.pilgrimhouse.co.kr.

Schmidt, Gary D. *John Bunyan's Pilgrim's Progress: A Retelling*. Illustrated by Barry Moser. Grand Rapids: Eerdmans, 1994.

Simpich, David. *The Pilgrim's Progress*. The David Simpich Marrionettes. Performed in Simpich Showcase Theatre, Mar. 18–Apr. 15, Apr. 29–May 14, 2016. Colorado Springs, CO, 2016.

Skwire Routhier, Jessica, et al. *The Painters' Panorama: Narrative, Art, and Faith in the Moving Panorama of Pilgrim's Progress*. Lebanon, NH: University Press of New England, 2015.

Taylor, Helen L. *Little Pilgrim's Progress*. Illustrated by Joe Sutphin. Chicago: Moody, 2021.

Van Halteren, Tyler. *Little Pilgrim's Big Journey*. Canada: Lithos, 2020.

Wright, Kenneth R., and Wayne Scott. *Pilgrim's Progress*. LifeHouse, ©2005, ©2019, Performed at LifeHouse Theater, Redlands, CA, Mar. 30–Apr. 28, 2019.

8

Margins

> Whoever heeds life-giving correction
> will be at home among the wise.
> Those who disregard discipline despise themselves,
> but the one who heeds correction gains understanding.
>
> Proverbs 15:31–32

I saw in my dream that Researcher was tidying up some of the materials on his desk. It looked like the Pilgrimverse adventure was coming to a close. As I looked, I saw two men jump out of a portal just out of Researcher's eye line. One was a very welcome sight, indeed, the other, not so much.

Christian: Hello, Researcher, I've heard a lot about you. Nice to meet you! I'm Christian.

RES: Why, hello, Christian. That truly is a lovely coat you're wearing. I've read a lot about it.

CHR: Let me introduce my companion here, Ignorance.

RES: Hello, Ignorance.

IGN: Hi there.

RES: I didn't expect you two to be hanging out together.

CHR: It's true that we parted on a clear disagreement near the end of Part I.

IGN: And, let's be honest, my parting from the book, as the warning climax, was dramatically final.

RES: Yes, being bound hand and foot and delivered by Shining Ones into the gates of hell is about as final as it gets.

IGN: Except there are plenty of versions of *The Pilgrim's Progress* where that doesn't happen to me at all!

CHR: In fact, there appear to be a host of reasons why Ignorance here experiences a varied reception in the Pilgrimverse. We can tell you more about these, if you're interested.

RES: I am interested. And I think you both can do me a favor. Much of our exploration has been a celebration of the Pilgrimverse. We've been touristy, for sure. Hopefully not too rose-tinted in our attention. But I am aware that there must be more critical and revisionist areas of the Pilgrimverse that have been something of a no-go zone so far.

CHR: That's right, there is a critical edge to the Pilgrimverse where Bunyan's text, theology or ideology is thought to need correction or improvement.

IGN: Some of this comes in relation to the distance in time of the original from a future readership. Adapters suppose their later rewrites are conjuring the spirit of Bunyan for their own age and its problems.

CHR: And others just don't like Bunyan's theology so that their revisions are corrective of what they see as untrue assertions of gospel truth.

IGN: And let's not forget that the earliest critical revision was by a TS, assumed nowadays to be a Baptist pastor named Thomas Sherman, who in 1682...

CHR: That's just a few years after Bunyan and Ponder published Part I!

IGN: Right, well, TS publishes a blatant knock off imitation, but in much more laboriously florid language. Supposedly an improvement for the cultured reader, it is one turgid tome!

CHR: A similar sort of thing is going on in Jim Pappas Jr.'s "New Amplified" version. The Californian author and playwright fleshes out the text in his modernization so that, for instance, at the cross Christian receives the seal as a branding with a glowing iron that threatens to painfully burn him. Christian is reassured that he needs to be marked by the subsequent scar, and then, mercifully, finds that the branding doesn't hurt much at all, because, the Shining One tells him, Jesus had already borne his pain for him on the cross.

IGN: That's quite an elaboration. But back to T. S., some think and Bunyan suggests in his introduction to Part II, that fraudulent copy-cat editions were a major impetus for Bunyan to write his own sequel.

RES: Well, you guys seem to know quite a lot already, why don't you just go ahead and explore the edges of the Pilgrimverse.

CHR: Well, to be honest, we anticipated this need for your project so we've done the exploration already and are all set to report.

RES: Impressive. Where do you want to start?

IGN: How about we start in a counterintuitive way? We could mention some of the ways in which *The Pilgrim's Progress* is received with correction from those who think Bunyan's theology in the text is good but lacking. They think it's not sufficiently orthodox.

CHR: Or not biblical enough, right? Remember how some editions and adaptations supplement Bunyan's marginal Bible references with additional references that implicitly do a better, more supportive job of authorizing the text.

IGN: Yeah, so Aneko Press put the fully transcribed Bible references directly into the text of the book, marked out by parentheses. But at the cross, for example, they substitute out Bunyan's Mark 2:5 reference for Isaiah 53:5.

CHR: In fairness, they do keep Mark 2:5 in the footnotes.

IGN: True. But back to Isaiah 53:5. The same verse crops up inscribed on the cross in the Chinese Graphic Novel by Tung and Wong.

CHR: It's like they're saying that Bunyan wasn't wrong, but he could have been more right with a more theologically appropriate Bible verse.

IGN: I think so. These kinds of moves indicate that the reception that matters is of the truth in the text and not the original form or explicit intention of the author. So Bunyan's choice of paratextual support in the margins can be corrected or supplemented in deference to the biblical truth.

CHR: C. J. Lovik has taken this the furthest with his book, *The Sojourner's Adventure Through Pilgrim's Progress*. Asking himself in his Foreword,

"Can Bunyan's Pilgrim's Progress be improved upon?" Lovik answers, "yes and amen!" His book is an allegorical account of conversations between Great-Heart, his daughter Fidelity, cousin Constance and a character called Faithless. The story of Pilgrim's Progress is told as Faithless has received it in a dream, but in a better order, according to Lovik's sense of the gospel. Along the way he provides a thematic concordance after each chapter showing the full text of supportive Scriptural verses and the text to which they are best connected. He calls these "concordance" sections, "Lighting the Pilgrim's Path with the Lamp of God's Word."

IGN: There's even a nice added touch of pastoral concern around the narrative of Doubting Castle, where Lovik adds an extra chapter, breaking his set format, on "Biblical Keys That Unlock the Chains of Doubt and Despair! Verses that every Christian should know as they make their pilgrimage to the Celestial City."

RES: So these additions are by authors who understand themselves to be supporters of traditional Pilgrimverse theology, right?

CHR: Yes. One really recent example is Peter Northcutt's translation of Part I which boasts the fullest compilation of Bunyan's bible references and allusions in its footnotes.

IGN: And I'd say this is one of the best re-writings to contemporary novelistic prose that we came across. Yes, a few of the longer theological conversations are cut and relocated to the Modern Saints series website, but the subtle changes come in small ways in the index.

RES: How so?

CHR: Well, the Bible references the edition supplies are not always those Bunyan pointed to, whether directly or indirectly, but have to do with the wording used in the rewrite that directs the biblical imagination elsewhere. No less biblical, we might venture, but just not Bunyan biblical!

IGN: And then there are the little tweaks. As so often, one to look out for is how the Man in the Iron Cage is dealt with. Gone is his report that God denies him repentance . . .

CHR: Whatever that might mean . . .

IGN: Granted, but in its place is the gentler suggestion that the man no longer hears God's call.

CHR: Yes, this does strike a different note, even if it gestures at the same idea. Which reminds me that another interesting glimpse we had, at the margins of the Pilgrimverse, was on insertions to the narrative that were corrective of a theological deficiency.

RES: What do you have in mind?

IGN: Are you thinking about baptism?

CHR: You got it! So, we found that there's dispute about whether the bath of sanctification at the Palace Beautiful in Part II is meant to be a representation of water baptism.

IGN: But, like, whatever, because Part II is barely acknowledged in these margins of the Pilgrimverse.

CHR: Right, so we found that, for example, a late eighteenth-century French translation gives a Catholic twist on Bunyan, and has a pool of penitence in which Christian must dip in repentance before he loses his burden at the cross.

IGN: Then in the mid-nineteenth century an Anglican adaptation for kids does the same thing, only here the baptism is located at the Interpreter's house.

CHR: And then, at the beginning of the twenty-first century, the very evangelical Protestant NavPress publish Lael Arrington's modernized retelling, and she too adds a baptism-type scene which unlike the Anglican order doesn't come before the cross.

IGN: Actually, Arrington's portrayal is a great way to illustrate how changing theologies of conversion change interpretative adaptation. In her account Christian comes to the Narrow Gate which opens for him. He walks through rather than being pulled through and immediately ascends a hill to the cross. His burden falls off and then he washes himself clean in a handy pool before receiving gifts from the Shining Ones.

RES: So, conversion is a free response tied immediately to the cross, forgiveness of sin and assurance, that is followed by voluntary baptism?

CHR: Yes. But there's more. Because, in fact, changing sensibilities see Pilgrim's Progress being used as a device for critique in a number of ways. For example, Nathaniel Hawthorne satirizes the easy, undemanding cultural Christianity that he saw around him in mid-nineteenth-century

America, by imagining a *Celestial Railroad* which turns out to be heading to the wrong eternal destination (spoiler alert!).

IGN: At roughly the same time, Harriet Beecher Stowe is setting the masses against slavery in her runaway success *Uncle Tom's Cabin*. Which is worthy of note at the edges of the Pilgrimverse, not only because she quotes from Pilgrim's Progress explicitly twice, and has narrative elements that echo Bunyan—not least a river crossing...

CHR: And she is quoting from Part II!

IGN: I was just about to say that!

RES: I happen to know that George Cheever, who edited, annotated, and wrote his own spin on a Pilgrim's Progress allegory was, himself, a very vocal abolitionist.

CHR: And did you know that William and Ellen Craft, a married couple, escaped their enslavement and wrote about it in their narrative, *Running a Thousand Miles for Freedom*?

IGN: And they do actually make their escape by train!

CHR: They make the case for their dignity and freedom for abolitionists with the help of several direct references to Pilgrim's Progress, not least in comparing the experience of pulling into Philadelphia as that of Christian feeling his burden fall from his back at the cross.

IGN: And this also makes the adaptations of the early 2010s for explicitly black urban readers worth noting. Judah Ben's *Kairo* and *Kairo Returns* for teen readers, and Jacqueline Busch and Melvin Patterson's *Christian's Quest* for upper elementary readers, set their stories and illustrations in modern urban contexts. Ben replicates street patois, while Busch and Patterson write of the young football player who is led to put aside sports glory for a higher calling, affected by the death of his grandfather. He leaves D'City for the Celestial City, and meets Mr Worldly-Wiseman...

IGN: And his dress sense replicates "Mike in his *Smooth Criminal* video."

RES: Mike?

IGN: I thought I was the ignorant one! Michael Jackson, dummy!

RES: Oh, right. Yes. Go on.

CHR: It can seem like the Pilgrimverse is overwhelmingly white, but actually, in the English-speaking world that's starting to change.

RES: And that change has been underway for a long time in respect to reception of the book in Africa. It's been so well documented by Isabel Hofmeyr in her *Portable Bunyan* that we don't have to cover it here. But it is a good reminder for us that we've limited our Pilgrimverse explorations to English. And, pertinent to your point, Christian, I remember Hopeful's transformations from the graphic novel realm of the Pilgrimverse.

IGN: And illustrations, like Patterson's, for example, have a strong role to play.

CHR: Yeah, that's why we liked Paul and Stephanie Cox's small children's book, *The Pilgrim's Progress: A Poetic Journey*. Without any big ado, Christian and his family are brown skinned, not at all part of the illustration tradition, but not at all distracting from telling the story.

RES: So racial awareness is a reality at the margins of the Pilgrimverse. How about gender? I'm thinking back to Hopeful's transformations again.

IGN: Glad you asked. It turns out that a load of adapters in the Pilgrimverse are women.

CHR: You might say that Pilgrim's Progress is most clearly established authoritatively in the domestic sphere of femininity and childhood in the use that Louisa May Alcott makes of the story to structure her *Little Women*.

IGN: The girls play at Pilgrim's Progress in the opening pages, and then chapter titles are drawn from Part I.

RES: We've explored the flavor of children's adaptation a little already in the Pilgrimverse Home conversation with James and Phebe. But I hadn't noted that aspect.

CHR: Helen Taylor's nineteenth-century children's version is still getting republished in the twenty-first century. Prolific British children's writer Enid Blyton had her own version, *The Land of Far-Beyond*. Jean Watson and Linda Parry add, serially, to these children's editions, with more than one edition each.

IGN: And then, we get the gender switching within the book. So, versions for kids often have the journey undertaken by a boy and a girl together, like Christian and Hope in Chariot Victor Publishing's *Christian's Journey*.

CHR: And Hopeful becomes female in a number of recent adaptations. But more distinctive still is Revelation Media's use of Kristyn Getty as the voice for the female Interpreter character in the 2019 CGI movie.

IGN: Yeah, that was a bold move for a character often associated with the Holy Spirit, or at least, as representative of an authoritative teacher of doctrine.

RES: You mean, because many fans of Bunyan's theology would not have women in the role of teacher, they will be still less comfortable with representing God as in any way female?

CHR: Right. Just search online for the controversy over female representation of the Trinity in an allegorical successor to Pilgrim's Progress, at least according to Eugene Peterson's blurb, in William Young's *The Shack*.

IGN: Let's pull back from that rabbit hole to note how the character of Faithful also becomes female at the edge of the Pilgrimverse.

CHR: Right. That's the case in Busch and Patterson's *Christian Quest*.

IGN: And did you know that his book actually grew out of a mural project that occupied an entire corridor of the building that housed an after-school program in downtown Chicago?

CHR: What's your point?

IGN: Just that that image, in black and white in the book, but in color in the mural, of a young black girl tied to the stake to be burned for her faith was the most arresting panel of the mural for many of the school kids, and especially as a heroic encouragement to the young girls who walked by.

CHR: Thanks for mentioning that.

IGN: The other female Faithful takes us further into critical waters.

RES: How so?

IGN: Steven Case's *This Road Tonight* is a satirically composed retelling. Christian meets Faith in the Valley of the Shadow of Death Mall. She, in fact, rescues him from the zombie shoppers and the VSDM employee, Neville.

CHR: I will fear Neville. Get it?

RES: Huh?

CHR: I will fear Neville. Psalm 23. I will fear no evil?!

RES: Arghh! Actually . . . that is funny.

IGN: This is besides my point. The point here is that Faith makes clear that instead of a burden, she bore a brand, a big letter "L," that she loses at the cross. She also makes it known to Christian that she is into girls. The L stands for Lesbian, but this is not a barrier to her joining the way to the City of Lights.

CHR: Without making a big deal about it, Case makes the case for gospel grace for Faith just the way she is. And then this is pursued further with the rendition of the Talkative character, as Chatter. Chatter is offended by the logo on Faith's T-shirt "Jesus Called. He Wants His Religion Back." And then when he learns of Faith's sexuality, we have a set piece conversation where the bigoted Bible-basher throws out verses from Leviticus and Romans which are parried with interpretations locating the verses as prohibitions of temple prostitution.

IGN: This isn't the place to rehearse those arguments. But Case's critique of conservative evangelical morality is deliberately framed as cold and pedantically rationalistic in making the conservative position represented by Talkative.

CHR: Yes, he's the religious know-it-all who does not know about the work of grace in his soul, according to the logic of Bunyan's original.

IGN: It's worth noting the range of Bunyan's appeal, that substantial differences in biblical interpretation of sexuality get aired as biblical exegesis in an adaptation of his most famous book. This, in itself, is quite a commendable testimony.

CHR: Another example that holds out grace against judgmentalism in regard to sexual behavior is a poignant poem by Stephen Kampa "Reading *Pilgrim's Progress* While Waiting to be Tested for STDs."

IGN: We won't quote it here, for copyright reasons, and I know giving the gist of a poem supposes the poem isn't the thing itself, but maybe it's enough to say that the protagonist of the poem seeks STD testing to reassure his steady girlfriend while the medical provider snidely assumes it is to check up on the effects of his ultra-libertine sexual promiscuity. The connections to the Pilgrimverse are precisely in challenging the fundamentalist and moralizing posture adopted in encounters where a person assumes from the surface details that they know about a person's inner life or motivations, a posture ascribed to you, Christian, by some critics.

CHR: A sympathy disconnect with Bunyan's allegorizing, perhaps? But still a powerful critique of judgmentalism that the poem's protagonist finds in *The Pilgrim's Progress*.

RES: Thanks. Ok, so we've seen race, gender, sex and sexuality at the edges of the Pilgrimverse. I must say that I was intrigued by the zombies—what else is in the range of alternative settings out there?

CHR: I'm so glad you asked! Did we mention that we found Sci-fi and fantasy adaptations? And, before this definitely gets us back into the male inflected area of the Pilgrimverse, I have to record here that one of the editors of the Aneko Press *Pilgrim's Progress*, Donna Sundblad, is also the author of *The Inheritance*. It's a fantasy tale of Jejune who leaves his home in Lofty Thought to seek truth, only to find that the villages along River of Tradition won't offer the pilgrim citizenship in the eternal city. His only option is the Narrow Way.

IGN: Another example is Steven James's Young Adult fantasy story, *Quest for Celestia*. It follows two teens, Kadin and Leira who have become aware of their disfiguring disease that gives them an ugly, stinking growth on their neck, which they share with fellow citizens of Abbadon. But none of the other residents perceive their owns sores, nor believe that relief is possible by seeking the mysterious Celestia over the mountains.

CHR: What works here is the pacing, the sympathetic characters, and, as an adaptation, the well-conceived inclusion of parallel narrative events.

IGN: It also means, and this is true of many adaptations, that the narrative coherence is important so that the kind of preaching that Bunyan breaks into via conversation is much less interruptive of the plot.

CHR: You mean, unlike the way we seem to be operating for Researcher's "Pilgrimverse Project?"

NAR: I heard that!

IGN: It's worth recognizing that recent innovations in publishing have made small scale self-publishing much more financially viable. A number of products at the margins of the Pilgrimverse emerge from this free-for-all in words devoted to defending, extending or rebutting Bunyan's story.

CHR: Can I talk about my favorite recent fun adaptation? It's called *Pilgrim's Progress Reloaded* and it's a sci-fi version. It originates in a podcast series. It may not work for every reader, but this tag line for the book back cover definitely intrigued my inner teenager: "Pilgrim's Progress is a classic allegory. It's also a story with no robots, space marines, or talking platypuses. So we fixed that. You're welcome."

IGN: We weren't convinced initially as the podcast audio is a little clunky in the voicing and pacing, but *Reloaded* is a great, page-turning read!

CHR: We should recognize that while some adaptations just modernize language, and some have Christian walking in more contemporary settings, sometimes even driving, this sci-fi rendition creates a wholly different world of intergalactic action. Christian is a space marine whose high-powered and extremely heavy armor is disabled by the unexpected activation of a tiny bot conscience who messes with his hardware. Before shooting Evangelist to death, he is given a holographic device that turns out to be a highly sarcastic Bible, touchy about how little she is consulted throughout the journey.

IGN: My favorite adaptation is the character of Law who turns out to be an indestructible and endlessly divisible sniper attack droid—even more trigger happy than Christian's companion, Zealot, who shoots first and asks questions later.

CHR: Having mentioned the varied reception of the Man in the Iron Cage, Umstaddt has fun devising a plot that throws biker Arminians and Calvinists into gang turf opposition.

IGN: The plot thrives on the ridiculously high body count of a shoot'-em-up video game but doesn't lose sight of importance of love and relationships, and, remarkably, a very clear moment of grace and forgiveness at the cross along the way.

CHR: The author even has fun inserting himself as the dreaming narrator in the final chapter and turning his humor on himself.

IGN: The charm of *Reloaded* is the framing of deep theological truths in narrative silliness. The parody professionals of the Christian web, Kyle Mann and Joel Berry of *The Babylon Bee*, offer their own *Postmodern Pilgrim's Progress*. And it's fair to say that it is just a bit more knowing in its humor.

CHR: Yes, there are abundant cheese jokes, but also chapter openings with epigraphs by T. S. Eliot, Nietzsche, Chesterton and C. S. Lewis. I reckon the characters of the Hollow Ones emerge from the hollow chested men of Lewis's *The Abolition of Man*.

IGN: And that's also the problem with tongue-in-cheek-parody—unless you are in the know many of the jokes can pass you by. Like many did me, in this version. On the other hand, I did appreciate the chapter opening quote from *The Princess Bride*!

CHR: I knew you'd mention that. The story is set in the parallel universe that a young man is thrown into by a cosmic accident involving a plummeting, ceiling mounted digital projector.

IGN: We are invited to sympathize with Ryan/Christian as we learn that his brother has recently died of cancer.

CHR: The struggle of the journey, his companions, and his destination in the dying lands serve overall as a parable calling him to faithful living once returned to his own dimension.

IGN: He doesn't get all his questions answered on his own terms, like the why of his brother's death, but he does get re-oriented. But, as with these creative adaptations, the fun is often in the details that will appeal to some and not others.

CHR: While we're on fun, can we just comment on Christiana's considered response to the inveigling of Mr Worldly-Wiseman in Kenneth Wright and Wayne Scott's musical production for the LifeHouse theater.

IGN: Oh yes, I love this.

RES: Do we have time?

CHR: Absolutely. She marches her quarreling kids up to him. He tries to introduce himself and she just says "Aww, Shut up!" and moves right on! Brilliant!

IGN: Just one more full adaptation. Let me preface this one by offering this suggestion: one way to praise an adaptation, in my reckoning, is if the plot works so well that you forget you are reading an adaptation.

RES: Just this one more, then. Tell me.

IGN: I'm thinking of *The Blood Miles* by Andrew Moody. Chris Walker is the pilgrim of this tale, who starts the story as the fill in sniper who has to take out the marauding truck of Savages. All is not what it seems in his community, however, and he soon leaves on the heels of Agent Veracis, (Evangelist(ic)) seeking a cure for the Tox (sin) that affects the population. With towns like the scientific Gaia or the hair-splitting humanists of Ockham contemporary worldviews are explored, but the adventure takes center stage. There's a mountain range with a pass called Wicket Gap that leads to the Crux (cross). In this post-apocalyptic, dystopian world of cover-ups and coercion, Chris is invested in making his way to the Central City.

CHR: The nods to Bunyan look pretty blatant to me.

IGN: But actually, if you were to read *The Blood Miles* without knowing *The Pilgrim's Progress* the plot would work well enough for you not to think of it as an adaptation at all.

RES: So then, in some way, a later reading of *The Pilgrim's Progress* could end up reminding you of *The Blood Miles*, right?

IGN: Yeah, that's what I appreciate.

CHR: That feeling of forgetting you're reading an adaptation is not what I got from *The California Pilgrim*. Now admittedly, the style of writing from the 1850s doesn't flow so well, but it is also belabored with moral judgment on the short-comings, from drinking to sabbath-breaking, of prospecting carpet-baggers who look likely to permanently upset the progress toward abundance of this promised land on the Western shore of the United States.

IGN: It's very topicality, commenting on the Sacramento fire of 1852, for example, is also what dates it, in ways that could just as well come to apply to later adaptations.

CHR: Quite so. Oh, but we should also mention here the sequels.

RES: Mnason, Gaius and Great-Heart mentioned Part III in our Pilgrimverse Books report.

CHR: That has to be the most enduring of sequels just because it was being printed and bound alongside Parts I and II long after publishers were openly acknowledging that it, in fact, was not written by Bunyan at all.

IGN: Right, and in fact we don't know who wrote it. But it's style is pretty different both in writing and in theological orientation.

RES: How so?

CHR: Well, let me give you an example: Goodwill gives the main character on pilgrimage, Tender-conscience, a crutch, and its description is far more ornate than Bunyan would have written it. It is made of "lignum vitae," Latin for the tree of life.

IGN: And then we read that the crutch sends "forth a certain odiferous perfume"! This is just one example where the register of vocabulary is elevated to rather ponderous artistry.

CHR: Also, Tender-conscience journey broadly takes the same path of Parts I and II, but there are differences. At the cross he ends up choosing between two houses, the House of Mirth and the House of Mourning.

IGN: Following Ecclesiastes 7:2, "It is better to go to the house of mourning, than to go to the house of feasting," T-C avoids the temptation of the former and heads to the latter to be congratulated by two matrons of the place.

CHR: In this house of good behavior, then, T-C prays and the Shining Ones show up to give him his threefold gifts, but not at the foot of the cross.

IGN: In fact, the whole point of the two houses being equidistant from the cross is to make the point that some are claiming allegiance to the cross but not walking the walk befitting its witness.

CHR: This makes Part III a religious manners book: Temperance and Health are added to Palace Beautiful to commend moderation, one of the key words of the book. Spiritual-man guides more pilgrims along with T-C in the ways of proper prayer and public worship, refuting a character called Human Reason along the way.

IGN: Gone is the radical dissenting spirit of kicking against social constraints, and the dynamism of the spiritual battle. Vanity is back to being as bullying as it was in Part I, such that the pilgrim called Yielding is enticed to leave the company and head to the pub where he drinks himself to death that very night!

CHR: It's certainly a more moralizing end than Faithful's, right? I wonder if *The California Pilgrim* had Part III in mind?

IGN: What should be clear at this stage of your exploration of the Pilgrim-verse, Mr Researcher, is that Bunyan's own sequel, Part II, doesn't command the same love from adapters as does Part I. It is as if Part I is the only necessary template for spin off creativity.

RES: Except for Sunday mornings.

IGN: Pardon?

RES: Sunday mornings, Bunyan's gift of hymn-writers, you recall, much to the chagrin of Shepherd-Boy in the Pilgrimverse Sounds expedition, comes from Part II.

IGN: So it does. But that's just a snatch of text, not a tribute to the narrative as a whole.

RES: And except for at funerals.

CHR: What?

RES: I said, and except for at funerals.

CHR: Yes, I heard, but I'm not sure I know what you're talking about. Didn't you do this already with Shepherd-Boy and Valiant-for-Truth?

RES: Well, yes . . .

IGN: Are you just morbid because you're old?

RES: I'm actually not that old, it's just male pattern baldness. Anyway, this is not about me. I'm not talking about the hymn, "To Be a Pilgrim." Rather, the passage of Christian and Hopeful over the river to the celestial city does get used a lot, but the highest profile has been given to Mr Standfast's crossing speech, from Part II.

CHR: Well, are you going to remind us what he says?

RES: OK, here goes:

> This River has been a Terror to many; yea, the thoughts of it also have often frighted me. But now methinks I stand easy. My Foot is fixed upon that upon which the Feet of the Priests that bare the Ark of the Covenant stood while Israel went over this Jordan. The Waters indeed are to the Palate Bitter and to the Stomach cold; yet the thoughts of what I am going to and of the Conduct that waits for me on the other side do lie as a glowing Coal at my Heart.
>
> I see myself now at the end of my Journey. My toilsome Days are ended. I am going now to see that Head that was Crowned with Thorns and that Face that was spit upon for me.
>
> I have formerly lived by Hearsay and faith, but now I go where I shall live by sight, and shall be with him in whose Company I myself delight.

It was used at the funerals of the UK's Queen Elizabeth, the Queen Mother, and US President Ronald Reagan.

IGN: OK, that's quite high profile. And those are good words. Very moving.

CHR: Hmmm, but it's also not that easy to keep going now you've brought up funerals.

IGN: Yeah, that is a bit of a downer.

CHR: But, it does get me thinking that Bunyan's books don't quite end with death, do they?

IGN: Well, very nearly.

CHR: Exactly. That is to say that after the crossing the river of death there is entry to the Celestial City.

IGN: Um. Yes. I guess . . .

CHR: You see where I'm going here, Ignorance?

IGN: All right, I do. Celestial City for you, or Hell, for me. I was happy to not remember that.

CHR: As also is true for many adapters.

IGN: Yes, that's right! And that gives me some cheer.

CHR: In fact, it is an interesting question whether Bunyan's cheerful confidence in the doctrine of Hell and divine eternal punishment for Ignorance, who ignores the free and grace-driven good news of salvation in Christ, has not itself moved to the margins of the Pilgrimverse. Bunyan ends his narrator's dream with you, Ignorance, being carted off, bound hand and foot, to the gates of hell by a couple of Shining Ones.

IGN: But many adaptations don't like this ending. Some, like Helen Trimiew's adaptation for Great Commission Publications, will shuffle my fate forward so that your arrival, Christian, with Hopeful at the Celestial City gives the book a happy ending.

CHR: Gary Schmidt has you caught and taken off by demons even earlier, not long after you were first met, so that you never get to the River at all. And sometimes you seem to get lucky, if you'll forgive me, when there's no mention of hell at all, as in Helen Taylor's *Little Christian's Progress*. Taylor just has you committed "into the country of the Wicked Prince" who makes sure you can never leave.

IGN: That does sound less apocalyptic, for sure.

CHR: And there's a further, probably unintended, irony: Taylor has that Wicked Prince tell you that "If you had really wished to live with the King, you should have done exactly as He told you."

IGN: Huh? I don't get what's wrong with that?

CHR: Wow, you do earn your name, don't you? You ignore everything I try to tell you! Remember, you think you are saved by Jesus counting your good works as righteous, but I tell you it's not about your works at all, but trust in his work of righteousness on your behalf?

IGN: Oh, yes, that does ring some bells . . .

CHR: Look, I'm not sure if it's a consolation, others just cut out your demise completely—you are just left wandering on the wrong path. This is often the case with children's adaptations. Vossos's graphic novel cuts you and your fate out altogether. But Tung and Wong keep all the details, but give you a special treatment—they include your fate in the right place in their Manga version, but it alone of all the episodes of the story is given in text and not images. Is this pastoral reserve or theological doubt?

IGN: It certainly differs from the full flaming details of Choi's graphic novel! Oooooh!

CHR: And one last mention, Robert McKenzie writes a sequel that revolves around your character.

IGN: Well, technically, it's not me.

CHR: Whatever, his updating sequel is told from the perspective of a would-be believer, Seeker, on the King's road trying to catch up with Christian. Seeker accepts clothes and a certificate at the cross from Fakesheep and Falsehope.

IGN: He didn't know their names, in fairness to him.

CHR: And it turns out, on the name front, that Seeker, in this story, ends up reverting to his former name of Coexist. He even gets a job offer at the University of Modern Theology where Professor Longsuffering finds that students are no longer interested in taking his traditional orthodox Bible classes. That's because he is in competition with courses in deism, moralism, and therapeutic religion taught by Professor Self-Help.

IGN: All right, let's get this over with. Coexist does catch up with Christian in the end but ends up clinging to his belief in a loving God who would never condemn anyone to hell and therefore will surely forgive everyone.

CHR: Coexist only entertains the notion that he might be wrong after seeing me cross the river and then finds that the waters don't bring him to the same place.

IGN: Hell, again.

CHR: Very much so, yes.

IGN: All right, that's enough about me. It makes me uncomfortable. Can we actually cheer things up a bit?

CHR: Well, maybe we should mention another marginal strand of the Pilgrimverse. Do you remember that one Christian has to give up his sport? Young Chris in the urban, black, *Christian's Quest*? Well, it's not all hard work. There's a golfer's *Player's Progress* out there. But you really have to care about golf to stick with it. In fairness, it doesn't try to replicate Bunyan's story around a golf course. Author, Tim Philpott builds in a thorough study of wisdom through personification of the book of Proverbs along the journey touring golfers take to a mystical Hebridean ideal idyll of a golf course.

IGN: And for the hobbyist, railway enthusiasts don't have to cast back to Nathaniel Hawthorne since Chris Brown wrote his *Journey to Zion* featuring train travel from Wales through England and then the channel tunnel to Calais, the unlikely site of the last judgment. From there on to the Swiss Alps to connect to the train to Zion which takes a thousand years, in keeping with millennial readings of the Bible. Brown notes a disproportionately high number of passengers boarding from S. Korea and China. Now, it is also true that there is a train going to the wrong destination chosen by some fancy passengers with VIP entitlement, but Brown reassures readers that passengers from other religions might choose a different train than Christians and Jews, but that all trains in that land "are bound for Zion."

RES: A word from you two about appropriation? Is this an example?

CHR: No, I think Brown is working in a lot of Pilgrim's Progress details. It's an adaptation. But, to be honest, we've not talked about appropriation because it's kind of a no-man's land of the Pilgrimverse. There's debate about whether it belongs or is just beyond the borders.

Into the Pilgrimverse

IGN: What Christian means is that the title *Pilgrim's Progress* is used pretty promiscuously in writing of the widest variety with little to no sense of connection to the book beyond the fact that its title has shaped the cultural imagination.

CHR: So, for example, the first part of a two-volume biography of the contemporary artist David Hockney is subtitled *A Rake's Progress*. This itself is an allusion to the original artwork of that title by Hogarth which was itself an appropriative allusion to Bunyan's classic when first produced. Hockney had designed the set for an opera production of *Rake's Progress*.

RES: This does seem marginal indeed . . .

CHR: Quite, well, just to report that the second volume of the biography is subtitled *A Pilgrim's Progress*. But this is not a shift of life-story to religious conversion territory. Rather, the most that could make the title fit is the artist's progress in use of new technologies to produce art. But the title mirrors the first volume and so, kind of, fits.

IGN: There are a ton of memoirs and even academic articles that use the title that is central to the Pilgrimverse as a hanger from which every form of narrative progression they claim to represent can be hung. This is very much marginal Pilgrimverse territory.

CHR: A British political cartoon portfolio by Ben Jennings is named *A Snowflake's Progress*. It is self-confessedly a tribute to Hogarth in mapping destitution under a recent UK government. At the same time, one image of a bicycle courier carrying a huge burden, entitled "Get on your bike," carries visual echoes of Bunyan's background story that underlays Hogarth's motif.

IGN: But those echoes are insubstantial, and perhaps accidental. It's a little like referring to Vanity Fair today when Thackeray's novel and Condé Nast's glossy lifestyle magazine and the Oscar's after-party have thoroughly invaded that Pilgrimverse borderland.

CHR: Before we hand over, let's just recognize that you can eat or stay overnight at J. D. Weatherspoon's The Pilgrim's Progress Pub restaurant and hotel in Bunyan's home town of Bedford.

IGN: Or you can order Progress beer at Pilgrim Brewery, in Reigate, England.

CHR: Or eat the Pilgrim's Progress sandwich at Erik's chain of delicatessens in northern California.

CHR: If you're a man you can check into addiction rehab at the Pilgrim's Progress program in North Carolina.

IGN: And while you're there you could, I suppose, read the 1876 temperance booster, *Bunyan's Pilgrims Progress and Intoxicating Liquors*.

CHR: You can arrange your homeschooling in the South Shore, Massachusetts, through Pilgrims Progress Home School Association and Pilgrim Progress Academy.

RES: All right. I think I can safely stop you there. Thanks so much, both of you, for taking on that final Pilgrimverse adventure.

IGN: You're most welcome. It was nice to be helpful for a change.

CHR: I am concerned for how you'll wrap things up from here, Mr Researcher. Wouldn't you say things are just too wide in the Pilgrimverse at this end of the exploration?

NAR: Thanks, Christian, I'll take it from here.

CHR: Nice to hear your voice, Mr Narrator. You still dreaming plenty?

NAR: Evidently. So, like he asked, is the Pilgrimverse too expansive? What do you think, Mr Researcher?

RES: Well, I think I'll try a summing up response of all this exploration after a little sit down, but I like the orientation you gave us by framing this particular expedition with those words from Proverbs 15:31: "Whoever heeds life-giving correction will be at home among the wise."

NAR: Say more.

RES: It seems to me that adapters often think of themselves as presenting Bunyan's message in more up to date garb. As opposed to appropriators who are those who just borrow a title, or narrative device, without recognition or acknowledgement of the message. Retellings across diverse genres update language, theological expression, and even moral perspective, but all in the name of faithfulness to the spiritual good of salvation to which Bunyan was pointing.

NAR: I agree. We don't have to think that Bunyan would always love the result to think that the aim of reaching readers or viewers that would otherwise not be reached would be one he would approve of.

RES: Particularly if it draws their interest to the underlying story set out in the Bible.

NAR: And there will always be plenty to contend for in the various interpretations of Scripture, so it's no bad thing that some of those interpretations find their way into Pilgrimverse adaptations.

RES: I'll mention Peter Northcutt's "new translation" again here, because he makes a concerted effort to communicate the loving concern and attentiveness of Christian and his companions in their encounters and conversations.

NAR: That's a reaction to reading Bunyan's dialogues as novelesque conversations that then come across as harsh or blunt.

RES: Because they are often mostly delivery points for a good sermon, rather than instruction on how to make friends.

NAR: And Northcutt doesn't skip the firmness with which, for example, Christian opposes Ignorance in their closing conversation. But he is keen to remove the emotional freight of the text from what might be taken to be an angry "fundamentalist" mode.

RES: It's this that has most disturbed my students, I think. They are encouraged by the enactment of key doctrines but discomfited by the swift passing by of enemies. In part, it's because they are so convinced by Bunyan's realism that it's hard for them to lean back into the allegory that is defining true and false discipleship rather than mapping tactics for missions or evangelism.

NAR: And the appropriators?

RES: Well, they at least testify that Bunyan is not without witness, just supposing those with the barest cultural awareness of the title should ever come across the book or one of its many adaptations with time and curiosity to spare to engage it.

NAR: For some, the book's place among the classics of English Literature places it among forbidding texts of the cultural elite.

RES: And this, despite the fact that, when editing the text, we found relatively few words that were inexplicable and in need of glossing. But I admit, Bunyan's phrasing and syntax make him a more demanding read than he would have been at the time he first hit the presses with *The*

Pilgrim's Progress. So this, again, becomes a case for an adaptation standing in for, or, who knows, maybe paving the way for encounter with the text.

NAR: So there is wisdom in not reducing the Pilgrimverse to authorized and authentically seventeenth-century text facsimiles, and appreciating the diversity at the margins, even when this expresses criticism of Bunyan, his leanings or those of his modern day advocates.

RES: And, also with Proverbs' claim that "one who heeds correction gains understanding," I think that the margins of the Pilgrimverse help Pilgrimnauts to discern where they see the core of Bunyan's message to be. Readings lean in on social, economic, even political and class perspectives in the text, but it's impressive that the spiritual and religious core remains the main, if contested, thing.

CHR: Ok, we've just been listening in, but, "Pilgrimnauts"? Really? You've got through this much of the expedition and now you want to throw in this already rejected label for us, again?

RES: You don't like it? I'm sure Narrator could work back and fill it into previous expeditions.

IGN: It's terrible. Forget it.

NAR: Yeah, I'm not going to be doing that. "Pilgrimnauts" is still a definite no-no. Anyway, look, I think you're in danger of leaving yourself nothing more to say in our final conversation. Let's go find our helpers to congratulate them on a very thorough season of exploration.

Pilgrimverse Resources:

Arrington, Lael. *Pilgrim's Progress Today*. Colorado Spring, CO: NavPress, 2002.
Ben, Judah. *Kai'ro Returns*. Chicago: Moody, 2013.
___. *Kai'ro: The Journey of an Urban Pilgrim*. Chicago: Moody, 2013.
Benton, J. A. *California Pilgrim: A Series of Lectures*. Sacramento: Solomon Alter, 1853.
Brown, Chris. *A Ticket to Zion: A Pilgrim's Progress by Train*. Eugene, OR: Resource, 2021.
Bunyan, John. *The Pilgrim's Progress*. Edited by Donna Sundblad and Ruth Zetek. Abbotsford, WI: Aneko, 2014.
___. *The Pilgrim's Progress: A New Translation*. Edited by Peter Northcutt. Modern Saints, 2024.
Bunyan, John, and James Pappas, Jr. *The New Amplified Pilgrim's Progress*. Shippensburg, PA: Destiny Image, 1999.
Busch, Jacqueline, and Melvin Patterson. *Christian's Quest. An Urban Adaptation of Pilgrim's Progress*. Chicago: Moody, 2012.

Case, Steven. *This Road Tonight: A New Pilgrim's Progress*. Berkeley, CA: Apocryphile, 2014.

Cox, Paul, and Stephanie Cox. *The Pilgrim's Progress: A Poetic Journey*. Peterborough, Canada: H&E Kids, 2019.

Craft, William, and Ellen Craft. *Running a Thousand Miles for Freedom*. Mineola, NY: Dover, 2014.

James, Steven. *Quest for Celestia: A Reimagining of The Pilgrim's Progress*. Chattanooga, TN: Living Ink, 2012.

Jennings, Ben. "Get on Your Bike." From *A Snowflake's Progress*, exhibition, July 2024. https://ben-jennings.com/Snowflake-s-Progress.

Kampa, Stephen. "Reading Pilgrim's Progress While Waiting to Be Tested for STDs." *Sewanee Theological Review* 54:1 (2010) 73–75.

Lovik, C. J. *The Sojourner's Adventure Through Pilgrim's Progress*. N.p.: Rock Island, 2019.

Mann, Kyle, and Joel Berry. *The Postmodern Pilgrim's Progress*. Washington, DC: Salem, 2022.

McKenzie, Robert. *Seeker's Progress*. Kindle Direct Publishing, 2021.

Moody, Andrew *The Blood Miles*. Melbourne, Australia: Brightmettle, 2023.

Philpot, Tim. *Player's Progress: A Golfer's Journey to Wisdom*. Milford, OH: Chilidog, 2022.

Trimiew, Anna. *Pilgrim's Progress: John Bunyan's Classic Story Adapted for Children*. Suwanee, GA: Great Commission, 2014.

Umstaddt, David. *The Pilgrim's Progress Reloaded*. Flintlock, 2024.

Further reading with Mr Researcher's friends:

Garrett, Christopher E. "Other Pilgrims: Sequels, Imitations, and Adaptations of *The Pilgrim's Progress*." *International Journal of English, Literature and Social Sciences* 5:1 (Feb. 2020) 13–20.

Johnson, Galen K. "'Be Not Extream': The Limits of Theory in Reading John Bunyan." *Christianity and Literature* 49:4 (Jan. 1, 2000) 447–64.

Sim, Stuart, "Bunyan and His Fundamentalist Readers." In *Reception, Appropriation, Recollection: Bunyan's Pilgrim's Progress*, edited by Stuart Sim and W. R. Owens, 213–28. Oxford: Peter Lang, 2007.

9

Conclusion

I am a fellow servant with you and with your fellow prophets and with all who keep the words of this scroll. Worship God!

REVELATION 22:9

One last time I saw in my dream that desk that had housed so many portals to the expanses of the Pilgrimverse. Mr Researcher was clearing away piles of Pilgrimverse products.

NAR: What's next, Mr Researcher?

RES: To be honest, I have to catch up with my grading. My students have been making their own Magic Lantern images based on episodes from *The Pilgrim's Progress* and writing spiritual journals in Bunyan's allegorical style. They're fun to review.

NAR: That does sound fun.

Honest: Did I just hear someone calling my name?
    I saw an older gentleman appear slowly from behind the last remaining pile on the desk. He was accompanied by a younger man leaning heavily on crutches.

RES: I'm sorry. I'm rather tired. You must be the oldest pilgrim we've entertained, but, in all honesty, I'm afraid I can't think of your name.

HON: Well, you've said it enough times. I'm Mr Honest. Old Mr Honest, to some, and this is my friend, Mr Ready-to-halt.

RES: Well, you are very welcome, but I'm afraid you're a little on the late side. Our exploration of the Pilgrimverse is over.

Ready-to-halt: Oh, don't mind us. We're not really ones for adventures, anyway. Our pace is a little more sedate.

HON: Yes, in fact, I've felt pretty worn out just listening to the adventures when our fellow pilgrim have reported back. Although, don't get me wrong, I can still put up a good fight against a giant if I need to.

RES: Well that's good to know, in case we meet one, but I don't think that's very likely at this stage.

I, the Narrator, at this comment, coughed loudly, almost exaggeratedly.

RES: Hmm? Look, seeing as you're here, why don't you two help me sum up what we've found in our survey of the Pilgrimverse.

HON: As I'm old and curmudgeonly, would you mind if I first sum up what we didn't find?

RES (nervously): I naturally defer to my elders, um, so, yes, please, do.

HON: Don't worry, you all did a good job, but as the old one here I should acknowledge that a boom industry of nineteenth-century adaptations has been largely skirted over.

RTH: Yes, Mr Honest here was telling me that good old Mr Cheever wrote a nautical reframing of *The Pilgrim's Progress*, for example.

RES: That he did. And you're right to spot that omission. I guess we've leaned nearest to the present day, as I inhabit it with my students. That's probably the foremost reason, but there are others. Those adaptations have been treated in book chapters already. The *Oxford Handbook* covers some of this area. And Hofmeyr's *Portable Bunyan* covers the flurry of missionary translation for Africa in the same time period.

HON: What other reason do you have? Not all of us have access to academic libraries, you know. And those books end up being expensive for the general reader, however much of a Bunyan fan they might be.

Conclusion

RES: Well, that's another concern, we've ended up drawing attention to more accessible products of recent years to give evidence for the continuing endurance and even expansion of the Pilgrimverse.

RTH: And may I say that I think you've done a good job of not neglecting the margins. I speak as one who tends to be pushed to the margins myself, when the action starts to pick up.

RES: Thank you, Mr Ready-to-halt. I appreciate that.

HON: We also noticed that you didn't give attention to social media or the Pilgrimverse's internet dimension.

NAR: Well, Mr Researcher has written a little about this.

RES: And we might have gotten a report on that area of the Pilgrimverse, but I ended up being let down.

HON: What do you mean?

RES: Well, I had a couple of volunteers set off on an expedition, but the report never came in.

RTH: They came back but refused to tell you what they'd found?

RES: No, actually, as far as I know, they haven't come back at all.

HON: Who would let you down in this way?

RES: Well, I don't like to say.

NAR: It was Apollyon and Mr By-Ends. I'll say it.

RES: What can I say? They must have found themselves some entertainment they couldn't tear themselves away from.

HON: Well, I guess readers will have access to the internet and social media themselves to supply the lack. More's the pity!

RES: To be honest . . . Oh, I'm so sorry. Look, I'm just not really on social media. I know there's a Facebook page of daily posted *Pilgrim's Progress* extracts, and there are TikTok reviews. In fact, many of the movie productions or images of the Pilgrimverse can be sampled or watched in full online. That accessibility extends to older editions of books digitized for Google Books or Project Guttenberg which do not require special subscriptions or paywall access. I certainly know my own collection of Pilgrimverse products could not have come together and keep growing were it not for internet shopping possibilities.

RTH: So, you're saying the other expeditions were nothing more than internet trawls? I thought our friends had been actually travailing and traveling through the Pilgrimverse, not just slouching in couches browsing the Web!

HON: Ouch!

RES: No, I wouldn't say that. The existence of accessible material is a different thing than a focused exploration that your friends have helped with. We've certainly benefitted from online information, but you have to really taste and see a Pilgrimverse product in full rather than rely on a few images or descriptions online.

RTH: So, no fake news here, right?

RES: That's right. But if you want to read about the Pilgrimverse in case studies of particular websites, I've written an article on that very topic, as Narrator mentioned.

RTH: Of course you have!

RES: Well, look, the thing is, although portals made the expeditions seem rapid, there were hours of careful reading, viewing, and listening behind the summary conversations we had at the report stage.

HON: I'm glad to hear that.

Evangelist: Me too!

RES: Where did you come from?

EVA: Same place as these two. Well, not quite, as they're from Part II and I'm only really in the first half of Part I.

RES: Still. Welcome. Um, it's good to meet you. You do know we're pretty much done?

EVA: Yes, I know, but I had a feeling I might be helpful in a summing up capacity.

RES: OK by me. What's your take on things?

EVA: Well, naturally I'm drawn to any clarity and prominence given to the good news of salvation in Jesus Christ in the Pilgrimverse. And I think this extends beyond the missionary use and Bible studies that Christiana and Mercy explored and critiqued in the Church expedition.

RES: Go on.

Conclusion

EVA: I've been encouraged to see that from the heart of the original text of *The Pilgrim's Progress* to the margins of the Pilgrimverse a sense of proximity to the Bible and Christianity is maintained.

RTH: Yes, I agree. This is true whether the Pilgrimverse is being covered by high-flying academics in their clever books and journal articles or by graphic novelists or Sunday School teachers.

HON: That Bible-adjacent status of *The Pilgrim's Progress* goes a long way to explain why I've heard that there are at least another two graphic novelizations on their way to presses and market in the next year or so.

RES: The Pilgrimverse expansion just keeps on going.

EVA: And clearly the potential for Christian's story in Part I, sorry Mr Ready-to-Halt and Mr Honest, that potential to frame the Christian story of conversion and discipleship, still attracts the imagination of those already on the narrow path as a way of communicating it to those not yet on the path.

HON: There's still a little irony there, though, isn't there, Mr. Evangelist? You gave Christian a roll of Scripture and pointed him to the Wicket gate, whereas many in the Pilgrimverse give out Bunyan.

EVA: Aha! But there's the danger of this expeditionary approach to the Pilgrimverse. It might be easy to have gotten so focused on these worlds to forget that *Pilgrim's Progress* fans aren't, with the possible exception of Mr. Researcher, obsessive to the exclusion of all else.

RES: Hey! What do you mean?

EVA: I mean that just because you participate in the Pilgrimverse doesn't mean that you neglect the Bible for Bunyan, or your family for movie-making, or the gospel for seventeenth-century literature, or your social or political convictions for fantasist escapism.

RES: And, as a matter of fact, I teach other classes, and love my wife and kids, and serve in my local church in ways that have nothing to do with the Pilgrimverse.

HON: I'm glad to hear that, too. Look, let's get back to assessing what you all did find. I had only really thought about books in the Pilgrimverse.

RTH: Yes, I'd expected all the adaptations, especially the children's versions, but hadn't expected other aspects. Perhaps because of my own circumstances, I'd not given any thought to song, much less dance—even if I did manage to foot it quite well when we vanquished Giant Despair.

HON: You did indeed. I for my part, being a little older, loved the movement of the Pilgrimverse into audio formats for listening. My eyes are not what they used to be, so a continued engagement with the book beyond reading is appealing to me.

RTH: I love it that the Pilgrimverse exists in relation to a work that John Bunyan had to offer justification for when he published it. Its creativity, its allegorical fictionalizing of everyday experiences of spiritual life, and its scripting of realistic dialogue all anticipate the creativity of its reception and adaptation into other genres.

RES: I have to confess, and not just because you're here, Mr Honest, that it's hard to give a definitive assessment of the scope of the Pilgrimverse. On the one hand, low costs, advanced technology, and world-wide online sharing increasingly means the communication of Pilgrimverse products is truly global and often instantaneous. And its historic reach extends in translation far beyond the limitations of our mostly English language survey. On the other hand, it is impossible to know what the existence of these products means for consumption and actual engagement. Clearly physical objects made for sale imply an expectation of a market and a return on the investment, but even then, many of the publishers are not for profit operations whose balances may be made up in any number of ways in the whole.

RTH: It probably fits the profile of *The Pilgrim's Progress* as a popular godly gift in Pilgrimverse constituencies.

RES: I agree.

HON: So what do we do with all this information about the Pilgrimverse?

RES: Christians will, I think, want to pray that the diversity in genre and expression of all the many Pilgrim's Progress products ultimately contribute to glorifying God and encouraging Christians in their walk of discipleship.

NAR: What about the role of the Pilgrimverse for creatives or literary folk who don't consider themselves Christian? Or even activists who are inspired by the nonconformity on display by Bunyan's pilgrims and by Bunyan himself as an artisan and untrained preacher?

RES: I suspect that here, too, the Pilgrimverse can sustain prophetic vision that attests to the goodness, truth, and justice of the world in which those thoughtful engagers of Bunyan's work live.

NAR: I see you're trying to get us back to my opening verse prompt for this concluding conversation.

RES: Yes, for religious and non-religious participation in the Pilgrimverse, I still harbor a basically theological read of what it can mean to fruitfully engage, promote, and diversify Bunyan's legacy. Bunyan sets himself up as a prophetic figure in his use of the dreaming narrator. The visionary and dream interpreting prophet Daniel is highly popular among seventeenth-century Protestant preachers. Visions and dreams play a consistent part in the testimony of Christian, Hopeful and Christiana's testimonies, too. The spiritual authority and the democratic access to that authority accords with the last days role of the Spirit to empower prophesying—which is how many Puritans referred to preaching. Especially, we might suppose, that which is legitimated by the Spirit's calling even when ruled illegitimate by the government, as in Bunyan's own case.

NAR: And from which prison penalty for unlicensed preaching his Pilgrimverse is a direct result.

RES: Quite. So the wrap up of the biblical book of Revelation has brought readers to the Celestial City, but also leaves them in the company of fellow prophets, testing and tasting the preaching of God's word in those days before the final judgment. In other words, Bunyan's work bears fruit for so long as it accords with lives called out to be lived for God. And not only that, but also those lives drawn into his orbit, which may then reflect back to the Christian community what they have missed of the gospel truth in their too cosy reception.

NAR: So non-Christian participation in the Pilgrimverse can have spiritual effect even if not offered on those terms?

RES: I judge that to be possible. I would take it that the Holy Spirit can take up and use the skills, passions, productions of any, much as, to make a Bunyanesque kind of move, the Spirit uses the non-Israelite prophet Balaam to speak truth.

NAR: Are you turning Bunyan or his *Pilgrim's Progress* into the speaking donkey that keeps interpreters from heading in the wrong direction? 'Cos, I think you're losing me on this gospel sense—it's like when Faithful makes an analogy from his conversation with Talkative to the Levitical law on clean and unclean hooved animals. Not entirely convincing as biblical interpretation, I'd have to say.

RES: Well, even there, Bunyan has Christian bring the analogy back to the gospel sense of the apostle Paul's condemnation of those speaking prophetically without love from 1 Corinthians 13.

NAR: Fair enough. So your point, again?

RES: The Pilgrimverse is a fascinating phenomena that has blessed and encouraged Christians for centuries, and even led some to become Christians in refracting biblical truth to them. It has also called out tremendous scholarship and artistry of many who do not profess faith in Jesus Christ. Nevertheless, it's not theologically wrong to count those contributions as glorifying to God even if the creators had no such intent or were agnostic as to its validity.

NAR: Just earning a living, following a hunch, taking a commission, or revisiting a childhood memory.

RES: Indeed. And the test for the Pilgrimverse is ultimately the same as for prophecy itself. Test it, and look for its fruit in confession of Christ and lives oriented to moral goodness. And, by the way, this gives fellow prophets, like my explorers and I throughout this whole extended adventure, every right to critique the Pilgrimverse and Bunyan himself where his vision or that of his interpreters needs challenging.

NAR: Nice word.

At this, as I was beginning to awaken from my dream, I suddenly saw a giant loom up behind Mr Researcher. He had a red beanie over his dark hair, he sported a full beard and was wearing a red plaid shirt. Over his shoulder he carried an axe. I knew immediately, as the narrator, that he was a ginormous lumberjack.

Mr Honest clung to Mr Ready-to-halt who clung back, dropping his crutches, and Evangelist put himself in front of them, as if he would be able to withstand an assault by a Giant of this dimension. Seeing this reaction on the desk and noticing the light of his office dim in the shadow suddenly cast behind him, Mr Researcher turned around.

RES: Good grief! It's you! I was so pleased to have got so far without running into you again.

Conclusion

GIANT: Hullo, again. I do always seem to be intruding. It's just that lots of people, some of them your students, keep implicating me in this Pilgrimverse. It's not my fault. I just get sucked in.

EVA: You two know each other? We're not in danger?

RES: Not unless you're a tree. This is Paul Bunyan, the mythical American lumberjack. No relation to John. He has the misfortune of being mistakenly ascribed authorship of the Pilgrimverse's central text by many a student writing assignment. I don't even know, at this point, if it's even an autocorrect thing or an AI generated suggestion.

NAR: Well, this is awkward. I'd imagined a more dignified ending.

RES: You know very well that you planned this ending all along. And to be honest, I'm glad. I could use a hand sorting out my shelving of all this Pilgrimverse paraphernalia. You up for that, Paul?

It really was time to wake up. So, I shook my imagination free from the giant lumberjack, the slightly shorter than average sized Researcher, and the miniature 2-D figures of Evangelist, Old Mr. Honest and Mr. Ready-to-halt on the desk. It was time to collate the expedition reports to commit the survey to the press. I hope you, the reader, will receive this as a celebration and a critical, if partial, perspective. And, with innovation always jostling with faithfulness in the Pilgrimverse, who knows when I might be obliged to dream again so that Mr Researcher's investigations resume where we've left off.

Last Bit of Further Reading with Mr Researcher and Friend:

Brown, Sylvia. "Giving Away 'Good Books': Gifting Bunyan and the Reproduction of Dissenting Communities." *Bunyan Studies* 22 (2018) 63–83.

Draycott, Andy. "The Internet and Contemporary Evangelical Reception of *The Pilgrim's Progress*." *Bunyan Studies* 24 (2020) 93–113.

Acknowledgments

The idea for the dialogue format of the book didn't, funnily enough, come directly from Bunyan. Rather, it came from my favorite undergraduate reading in contemporary political philosophy, Daniel Bell's *Communitarianism and Its Critics* (Oxford, 1993). Having characters jump out of books is mostly inspired by Jasper Fforde's Thursday Next series, starting with *The Eyre Affair* (Hodder and Stoughton, 2001), as well as the eye-catching book sculpture by Justin Rowe of Christian and Hopeful arising out of the billowing pages of the river of death. The 2-D nature of the characters against a 3-D setting reverses the wonderful animation style of the BBC's *Paddington* with which I grew up.

My concentration on reception of *The Pilgrim's Progress* was almost very short-lived, arising as it did in relation to a class on "The Pilgrim's Progress and its Legacy," co-taught only once with Dr. Natasha Duquette. Some years later, the opportunity to develop a solo class for Biola University's Bible minor as an upper-level, general education Integration Seminar reignited my research and writing. A couple of Provost's Faculty Research Grants, a partial research leave, and a research sabbatical have provided funding and time to locate and gather Pilgrimverse products and then write about them. I am particularly grateful to Biola University Provosts Deborah Taylor and Matt Hall and Talbot School of Theology Deans Clint Arnold, Tim Pickavance, Ed Stetzer, Scott Rae, Doug Huffman, and the ever-encouraging Joanne Jung, and my chair, Uche Anizor.

Participation in the wonderfully welcoming space of the International John Bunyan Society was first encouraged and commended to me by Galen Johnson. His gracious advice and wisdom has been matched by the Society's collegiality. The Society, its journal, *Bunyan Studies*, the triennial conferences and the annual newsletter, *The Recorder*, have allowed me to develop my thinking and writing well beyond areas of my formal training.

I am grateful to feedback and advice from Bob Owens, Rachel Adcock, David Gay, and Richard Bergen. None of them, nor any of my anonymous blind peer reviewers, ever suggested I write as I have done in this book. That's all my own fault.

Previously published articles have bled into my writing of two chapters. I am grateful to the editors for their permission to rework material that appeared as "Iconoclasm, Iconophobia, and Graphic Novel Adaptations of John Bunyan's *The Pilgrim's Progress*," *Journal of Graphic Novels and Comics* 12 (2021) 964–92, for elements of chapter 3, and as "Missional Pilgrim's Progress in Memory of Her: Representing Women in Adaptations of a Classic," *Evangelical Missiological Society Occasional Bulletin*, Spring 2020 and as "Evangelical Devotionals and Bible Studies of *The Pilgrim's Progress*: Fidelity or Bibliolatry?" *Christian Education Journal: Research on Educational Ministry* 17 (2020) 264–82, for elements of chapter 4.

I finished writing this last chapter on the same day that Margaret Breen and I also submitted our manuscript of the Norton Library series edition of *The Pilgrim's Progress*. That two-year project has been an immense blessing of careful scholarly collaboration, affirming collegiality and growing friendship.

A year's worth of Biola University students, through spring, summer, and fall 2024, have been required to trudge through early drafts of this material. I have valued all of their comments, and often made changes to improve the text at their behest. They are my chief target readers. Weaknesses in the book remain fully my own.

I am grateful to my family for patiently bearing with the seemingly neverending flow of Pilgrim's Progresses delivered to our doorstep.

It would not have been possible to finish this project at a busy teaching university without the help of teaching assistants. To them, as well as to my students, I dedicate this book. Thank you Cole, Brianna, Emma, Emma, Ashley, Christopher, and Peyton.

To Siân, with love.

www.ingramcontent.com/pod-product-compliance
Lightning Source LLC
Chambersburg PA
CBHW070300230426
43664CB00014B/2591